CASSEROLES

Norma MacMillan

CHANCELLOR
PRESS

CONTENTS

First published in Great Britain in 1979

This edition published in 1994 by Chancellor Press
an imprint of Reed Consumer Books Limited
Michelin House, 81 Fulham Road, London SW3 6RB
and Auckland, Melbourne, Singapore and Toronto

Reprinted 1994

Copyright © 1979 Reed International Books Limited

ISBN 1 85152 515 7

A CIP catalogue record for this book is available from the British Library

Produced by Mandarin Offset
Printed and bound in Hong Kong

INTRODUCTION

What comes to mind when you see a casserole recipe in a cookery book? A piping hot, nourishing meal on a frozen winter's day? A sophisticated dinner party main dish? A simple way of experimenting with new and exotic cuisines? The casserole is all these, and more.

All kinds of ingredients can make up a casserole – fish, meat, poultry and game, vegetables, pulses, pasta, rice and cheese. And by its very nature, the casserole is simplicity itself: one pot cookery.

Most casseroles require little attention during cooking – they can be popped into the oven and simply forgotten about for an hour or so. With the aid of an automatic oven timer, you can return to a delicious ready-cooked casserole after a hectic day. And yet, not all casseroles take hours to cook: those prepared from leftovers and convenience foods can be ready in less than half an hour.

Whether you are feeding a hungry family or giving a dinner party you will find casseroles suitable for every occasion in this exciting new cookbook.

NOTES

Standard spoon measurements are used in all recipes
1 teaspoon = one 5 ml spoon
1 tablespoon = one 15 ml spoon
All spoon measures are level.

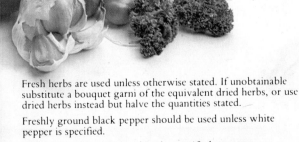

Fresh herbs are used unless otherwise stated. If unobtainable substitute a bouquet garni of the equivalent dried herbs, or use dried herbs instead but halve the quantities stated.

Freshly ground black pepper should be used unless white pepper is specified.

Ovens should be preheated to the specified temperature.

For all recipes, quantities are given in both metric and imperial measures. Follow either set of measures but not a mixture of both, because they are not interchangeable.

FISH & SHELLFISH

Whole Fish with Tomato Sauce

1 x 1.5 kg (3 lb)
    whole fish (bass,
    bream, brill, etc.),
    cleaned
2 tablespoons plain
    flour
salt and pepper
65 g (2½ oz) butter
1 onion, chopped
1 green pepper,
    cored, seeded and
    chopped
1 red pepper, cored,
    seeded and chopped
2 celery sticks,
    chopped
2 x 397 g (14 oz)
    cans tomatoes
1 tablespoon tomato
    purée
1 tablespoon
    Worcestershire
    sauce
1 tablespoon lemon
    juice
few drops of Tabasco
    sauce
1 bay leaf
parsley sprigs to
    garnish

Rinse the fish and pat dry with kitchen paper. Season the flour and rub this all over the fish, inside and out. Place the fish in a casserole or baking dish into which it fits snugly.

Melt the butter in a saucepan. Add the onion, green and red peppers and celery and fry until the onion is softened. Stir in the tomatoes with their juice, tomato purée, Worcestershire sauce, lemon juice, Tabasco and the bay leaf. Bring to the boil and simmer for 15 minutes or until the vegetables are tender.

Remove the bay leaf, then purée the sauce by rubbing through a sieve or working in an electric blender. Adjust the seasoning, then pour the sauce around the fish. Cook in a preheated moderate oven, 180°C (350°F), Gas Mark 4, for 45 minutes or until the fish is tender. Baste the fish frequently with the sauce during cooking. Garnish with parsley.
Serves 4 to 6

Prawns in Herb Butter

1 kg (2 lb) unshelled
   raw prawns
salt and pepper
1.75 litres (3 pints)
   water
125 g (4 oz) butter
2 tablespoons
   chopped parsley
3 tablespoons
   chopped fresh
   herbs as available
   (preferably
   tarragon and basil)
juice of ½ lemon
chopped parsley to
   garnish

Cook the prawns in lightly salted boiling water for about 5 minutes or until pink. Drain and allow to cool slightly, then remove the shells.

Cream together the butter, parsley, herbs, salt and pepper to taste and the lemon juice. Spread half the herb butter over the bottom of a flameproof baking dish. Press the prawns into the butter, in rows, and cover with the remaining herb butter.

Cook in a preheated moderately hot oven, 200°C (400°F), Gas Mark 6, for 10 minutes. Pop the dish under a preheated grill and cook for a few more minutes or until the top browns. Garnish with parsley.

Serves 4

NOTE: If raw prawns are unobtainable, substitute 500 g (1 lb) frozen, shelled prawns. Do not precook; simply thaw before adding to the herb butter.

Whole fish with tomato sauce; Prawns in herb butter; Mediterranean fish steaks (page 8).

Mediterranean Fish Steaks

4 tablespoons olive oil

2 onions, thinly sliced

1 clove garlic, finely chopped

1 green pepper, cored, seeded and sliced in rings

4 large tomatoes, skinned and sliced

2 teaspoons dried basil

salt and pepper

4 white fish steaks

2 teaspoons lemon juice

6 tablespoons dry white wine

Heat the oil in a frying pan and fry the onions and garlic until softened. Add the green pepper rings and continue frying for 3 minutes. Remove from the heat and place half the mixture in a casserole.

Arrange half the tomato slices on top and sprinkle with half the basil and salt and pepper to taste. Place the fish steaks on top and sprinkle with the lemon juice. Add the rest of the tomato slices, basil and onion and green pepper mixture. Pour in the wine.

Cover and cook in a preheated moderate oven, 180°C (350°F), Gas Mark 4, for about 45 minutes or until the fish is tender.

Serves 4

Illustrated on page 7.

Casseroled Shellfish

750 g (1 ½ lb) potatoes

salt and pepper

40 g (1 ½ oz) butter

2 tablespoons plain flour

175 ml (6 fl oz) milk

175 ml (6 fl oz) dry white wine

250 g (8 oz) canned crabmeat, drained and flaked

350 g (12 oz) frozen shelled prawns, thawed

1 small onion, grated

3 tablespoons chopped parsley

75 g (3 oz) Cheddar cheese, grated

watercress sprigs to garnish

Parcook the potatoes in boiling salted water for 10 minutes, then drain and slice thinly.

Melt 25 g (1 oz) of the butter in a saucepan. Add the flour and cook, stirring, for 1 minute. Gradually stir in the milk and wine and bring to the boil. Simmer, stirring, until thickened. Add salt and pepper to taste and fold in the crabmeat, prawns, onion, parsley and cheese.

Layer one third of the potato slices in a greased casserole. Cover with half the fish mixture. Repeat the layers, finishing with a layer of potato slices. Dot with the remaining butter.

Cook in a preheated moderate oven, 180°C (350°F), Gas Mark 4, for about 45 minutes or until the potatoes are tender and the top is crisp. Garnish with watercress.

Serves 4

Greek Prawn Casserole

300 ml (½ pint)
  water
juice of ½ lemon
1 kg (2 lb) unshelled
  raw prawns
3 tablespoons olive
  oil
1 onion, finely
  chopped
1 clove garlic,
  crushed
2 x 397 g (14 oz)
  cans tomatoes,
  drained and
  chopped
¾ teaspoon dried
  oregano
salt and pepper
75 g (3 oz) Fetta
  cheese, crumbled

Bring the water and lemon juice to the boil in a saucepan. Add the prawns and simmer for 5 minutes or until pink. Drain, reserving the liquid, cool slightly, then remove the shells. Boil the liquid until reduced to 150 ml (¼ pint).

Heat the oil in a flameproof casserole. Add the onion and garlic and fry until softened. Stir in the tomatoes, oregano, reserved prawn cooking liquid and salt and pepper to taste. Simmer until the sauce is reduced and thickened.

Fold the prawns into the sauce. Sprinkle the cheese on top and cook in a preheated moderate oven, 180°C (350°F), Gas Mark 4, for 15 minutes.
Serves 4
NOTE: If raw prawns are unobtainable, substitute 500 g (1 lb) frozen, shelled prawns. Do not precook; simply thaw and add them to the cooked sauce. For the cooking liquor use 150 ml (¼ pint) water and 2 teaspoons lemon juice.

Mullet Mornay

500 g (1 lb) spinach
salt and pepper
50 g (2 oz) butter
125 g (4 oz)
  mushrooms, sliced
750 g-1 kg (1 ½-2 lb)
  mullet or other fish
  fillets, skinned
40 g (1 ½ oz) plain
  flour
450 ml (¾ pint)
  milk
grated nutmeg
50 g (2 oz) Gruyère
  cheese, grated
50 g (2 oz) Cheddar
  cheese, grated
parsley sprigs to
  garnish

Cook the spinach, with only the water clinging to the leaves after washing, until tender. Drain well, pressing out all excess water, then chop. Season with salt and pepper to taste and stir in 15 g (½ oz) of the butter. Spread the spinach over the bottom of a greased casserole. Cover with the mushrooms and arrange the fish fillets on top.

Melt the remaining butter in a saucepan. Add the flour and cook, stirring, for 1 minute. Gradually stir in the milk and bring to the boil. Simmer, stirring, until thickened. Season to taste with salt, pepper and nutmeg, then stir in all but 2 tablespoons of the cheese.

Pour the cheese sauce over the fish and sprinkle the reserved cheese on top. Cook in a preheated moderate oven, 180°C (350°F), Gas Mark 4, for about 30 minutes or until the fish is tender. Garnish with parsley.
Serves 4

Herby Cod Casserole

500 g (1 lb) cod
  fillets
15 g (½ oz) butter
15 g (½ oz) plain
  flour
250 ml (8 fl oz)
  milk
¼ teaspoon garlic
  salt
¼ teaspoon dried
  thyme
¼ teaspoon dried
  oregano
6 spring onions,
  finely chopped
salt and pepper
paprika

Arrange the cod fillets in a greased
baking dish. Melt the butter in a
saucepan. Add the flour and cook,
stirring, for 1 minute. Gradually stir
in the milk and bring to the boil.
Simmer, stirring, until thickened.
Stir in the garlic salt, herbs, spring
onions and salt and pepper to taste.
Pour over the fish and sprinkle with
a little paprika.

Cook in a preheated moderate
oven, 180°C (350°F), Gas Mark 4, for
30 minutes or until the fish is tender.
Serves 4

Fish Boulangère

500 g (1 lb) potatoes
salt and pepper
50 g (2 oz) butter
1 clove garlic, very
　finely chopped
750 g (1½ lb) white
　fish fillets, skinned
　and cut into
　chunks
1 large onion, thinly
　sliced

Parcook the potatoes in boiling salted water for 10 minutes. Drain and slice thinly.

Cream half the butter with the garlic and spread over the bottom of a casserole. Arrange the fish chunks on top and sprinkle with salt and pepper. Cover with the onion and then the potato slices. Dot with the remaining butter.

Cook in a preheated moderate oven, 180°C (350°F), Gas Mark 4, for about 40 minutes or until the fish and potatoes are tender.
Serves 4

Haddock with Grapefruit and Mushrooms

4 haddock fillets,
　skinned
50 g (2 oz) butter
3 spring onions,
　chopped
salt and pepper
2 grapefruit
125 g (4 oz)
　mushrooms, sliced

Arrange the haddock fillets in a greased casserole. Mash the butter with the spring onions and salt and pepper to taste. Grate the rind from the grapefruit and beat into the butter. Spread this over the haddock fillets. Cover with the mushrooms.

Squeeze the juice from one grapefruit and peel and segment the other. Pour the grapefruit juice over the mushrooms and place the grapefruit segments on top.

Cover and cook in a preheated moderate oven, 180°C (350°F), Gas Mark 4, for about 30 minutes or until the fish is cooked.
Serves 4

Smoked Haddock au Gratin

*500 g (1 lb) smoked
   haddock fillets
milk for poaching
50 g (2 oz) butter
25 g (1 oz) plain
   flour
175 ml (6 fl oz)
   single cream
salt and pepper
50 g (2 oz) Cheddar
   cheese, grated
25 g (1 oz) fresh
   breadcrumbs
parsley sprigs to
   garnish*

Put the haddock fillets in a saucepan,
pour over enough milk to cover and
poach gently for 15 minutes. Drain,
reserving the milk, and flake the fish.

Melt the butter in a clean
saucepan. Add the flour and cook,
stirring, for 2 minutes. Gradually stir
in the cream and 175 ml (6 fl oz) of
the reserved poaching milk. Bring to
the boil, stirring, and simmer until
thickened. Season with salt and
pepper to taste. Stir in all but 1
tablespoon of the cheese and when it
has melted fold in the flaked fish.
Turn into a greased casserole.

Mix together the breadcrumbs and
remaining cheese and sprinkle over
the top. Cook in a preheated
moderately hot oven, 190°C (375°F),
Gas Mark 5, for 20 minutes or until
the top is golden brown. Garnish
with parsley.

Serves 4

Fish with Horseradish Cream

1 kg (2 lb) white fish
    cutlets
300 ml (½ pint) fish
    or chicken stock
1 tablespoon lemon
    juice
40 g (1½ oz) butter
40 g (1½ oz) plain
    flour
150 ml (¼ pint)
    single cream
1 tablespoon
    horseradish sauce
salt and pepper
chopped chives to
    garnish

Arrange the fish in one layer in a baking dish. Pour over the stock and lemon juice and cook in a preheated moderately hot oven, 200°C (400°F), Gas Mark 6, for 15 to 20 minutes or until almost cooked.

Drain off the cooking liquid into a saucepan; keep the fish warm. Boil the liquid until it is reduced to 150 ml (¼ pint).

Melt the butter in a clean saucepan. Add the flour and cook, stirring, for 2 minutes. Gradually stir in the reduced cooking liquid and bring to the boil, stirring. Stir in the cream, horseradish sauce and salt and pepper to taste. Pour this sauce over the fish and return to the oven. Cook for a further 15 minutes. Serve garnished with chives.

Serves 4

Salt Cod and Celery Bake

500 g (1 lb) dried
    salt cod, soaked
    overnight
40 g (1½ oz) butter
40 g (1½ oz) plain
    flour
450 ml (¾ pint)
    milk (or half fish
    stock and half
    milk)
pinch of dry mustard
salt and pepper
1 egg, beaten
125 g (4 oz) fresh
    breadcrumbs
4 celery sticks, finely
    chopped
tomato slices to
    garnish

Drain the cod and place in a saucepan. Cover with fresh water and bring to the boil. Simmer for 20 minutes, then drain well. Skin, bone and flake the fish.

Melt the butter in another saucepan. Add the flour and cook, stirring, for 2 minutes. Gradually stir in the milk (or stock and milk) and bring to the boil. Simmer, stirring, until thickened. Add the mustard and salt and pepper to taste. Remove from the heat and cool slightly, then beat in the egg.

Place half the cod in a greased baking dish. Cover with half the breadcrumbs, half the celery, then half the sauce. Repeat the layers.

Cook in a preheated moderately hot oven, 190°C (375°F), Gas Mark 5, for 20 minutes. Garnish with tomato slices.

Serves 4

Tuna Noodle Casserole

500 g (1 lb) noodles
salt and pepper
1 x 298 g (10½ oz)
  can condensed
  cream of
  mushroom soup
2 tablespoons
  medium sherry
2 x 198 g (7 oz)
  cans tuna fish,
  drained and flaked
6 spring onions,
  finely chopped
4 hard-boiled eggs,
  sliced
25 g (1 oz) crisps,
  crushed
2 tablespoons grated
  Parmesan cheese

Cook the noodles in boiling salted water until tender. Drain well, then mix in the soup and sherry. Put about one third of the noodle mixture in a greased casserole. Cover with half the tuna, spring onions and eggs, then season with salt and pepper to taste. Repeat the layers and top with the remaining noodle mixture.

Mix together the crisps and cheese and sprinkle over the top. Cook in a preheated moderate oven, 180°C (350°F), Gas Mark 4, for 25 to 30 minutes or until the top is golden brown.

Serves 4 to 6

Haddock in Cider

750 g (1½ lb)
  haddock fillets,
  skinned and cut
  into chunks
2 eating apples, cored
  and sliced
2 celery sticks,
  chopped
1 teaspoon chopped
  sage
salt and pepper
300 ml (½ pint) dry
  cider
15 g (½ oz) butter
15 g (½ oz) plain
  flour
parsley sprigs to
  garnish

Put the fish in a greased flameproof casserole and cover with the apple slices and celery. Sprinkle with the sage and salt and pepper to taste, then pour in the cider.

Cover and cook in a preheated moderate oven, 180°C (350°F), Gas Mark 4, for 25 to 35 minutes or until the fish is tender.

Transfer the fish and apple slices to a warmed serving dish and keep hot.

Blend the butter with the flour to make a smooth paste. Add a little of the hot cooking liquid, then stir this into the remaining liquid in the casserole. Bring to the boil on top of the stove, stirring, and simmer until thickened, then pour over the fish. Garnish with parsley.

Serves 4

Crab and Spaghetti Bake

175 g (6 oz)
  spaghetti
salt and pepper
25 g (1 oz) butter
1 large onion,
  chopped
1 medium red
  pepper, cored,
  seeded and diced
25 g (1 oz) plain
  flour
300 ml (½ pint)
  milk
150 ml (¼ pint)
  single cream
2 teaspoons French
  mustard
1 tablespoon
  Worcestershire
  sauce
250 g (8 oz) cooked
  fresh, or canned
  crabmeat, drained
  and flaked
4 hard-boiled eggs,
  sliced
125 g (4 oz) mature
  Cheddar cheese,
  grated

Break the spaghetti into short lengths and cook in boiling salted water until just tender. Meanwhile, melt the butter in a saucepan, add the onion and red pepper and sauté until softened. Stir in the flour and cook, stirring, for 1 minute, then gradually stir in the milk and cream. Bring to the boil and simmer, stirring, until thickened. Stir in the mustard, Worcestershire sauce and salt and pepper to taste.

Drain the spaghetti and fold into the sauce. Spread half this mixture in a greased shallow casserole. Cover with the crabmeat, then the sliced eggs and top with the remaining spaghetti sauce. Sprinkle the cheese over the top. Cook in a preheated moderately hot oven, 190°C (375°F), Gas Mark 5, for 25 minutes or until heated through and bubbling.

Serves 4 to 6

BEEF

Italian Pot Roast

1-1.25 kg (2-2½ lb)
   piece of beef
   topside
salt and pepper
3 tablespoons olive
   oil
1 onion, chopped
1 clove garlic,
   crushed
2 large carrots, sliced
2 celery sticks, sliced
1 x 227 g (8 oz) can
   tomatoes, drained
   and chopped
300 ml (½ pint) dry
   red wine
1 teaspoon dried
   oregano
1 bay leaf

Rub the beef all over with salt and pepper. Heat the oil in a flameproof casserole, add the beef and brown on all sides, then remove from the casserole.

Add the onion, garlic, carrots and celery to the casserole and fry until the onion is softened. Stir in the tomatoes, wine, oregano and bay leaf and bring to the boil.

Return the beef to the casserole and turn over in the liquid. Cover tightly and cook in a preheated moderate oven, 180°C (350°F), Gas Mark 4, for 3 hours or until the meat is tender. Baste occasionally during the cooking.

Remove the beef from the casserole, place on a warmed serving plate and keep hot.

Boil the cooking liquid on top of the stove until well reduced and thickened. Strain and serve as a sauce, with the beef.
Serves 4

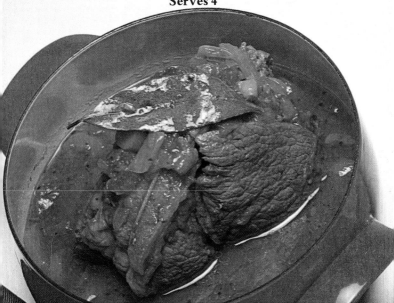

Italian Beef Casserole

2 tablespoons olive oil
1 onion, chopped
1 clove garlic, crushed
4 bacon rashers,
    derinded and diced
2 carrots, diced
1 celery stick, diced
500 g (1 lb) minced
    beef
1 x 298 g (10½ oz)
    can condensed
    tomato soup
1 x 397 g (14 oz)
    can tomatoes,
    drained
1 teaspoon dried basil
salt and pepper
250 g (8 oz) noodles
125 g (4 oz) Cheddar
    cheese, grated

Heat the oil in a frying pan, add the onion, garlic and bacon and fry until the onion is softened. Add the carrots and celery and continue frying for 3 minutes. Stir in the beef and brown well, then add the soup, tomatoes, basil and salt and pepper to taste. Cook gently for about 15 minutes.

Meanwhile, cook the noodles in boiling salted water until tender. Drain well. Add the noodles to the beef mixture and fold together, then turn into a casserole. Sprinkle the cheese over the top. Cook in a preheated moderate oven, 180°C (350°F), Gas Mark 4, for 30 minutes.
Serves 4

Beef Olives

1 kg (2 lb) piece of
  beef top rump, cut
  into 6 slices
salt and pepper
1 teaspoon dried
  thyme
12 thin slices of
  smoked ham
25 g (1 oz) butter
1 tablespoon oil
1 onion, chopped
300 ml (½ pint)
  stout
thyme sprigs to
  garnish (optional)

Pound the beef slices until they are thin, then cut each slice in half to make 12 slices, each about 12.5 x 9 cm (5 x 3½ inches). Rub each slice with a little seasoning and thyme, then place a slice of ham on each and trim to fit; reserve any trimmings. Roll up and secure with string.

Melt the butter with the oil in a flameproof casserole. Add the beef rolls and brown on all sides. Remove and set aside.

Add the onion to the casserole with any ham trimmings and fry until softened. Return the beef rolls to the casserole and pour over the stout. Bring to the boil, then cover and transfer to a preheated moderate oven, 180°C (350°F), Gas Mark 4. Cook for 1 hour or until the beef rolls are tender. Remove the string. Garnish with thyme sprigs and serve with carrots, if liked.

Serves 4 to 6

Beef and Spinach Bake

750 g (1 ½ lb)
    spinach
1 tablespoon oil
1 large onion, finely
    chopped
500 g (1 lb) minced
    beef
250 g (8 oz)
    mushrooms, sliced
150 ml (¼ pint)
    fresh sour cream
½ teaspoon dried
    oregano
½ teaspoon dried
    basil
½ teaspoon dried
    thyme
125 g (4 oz)
    Cheddar cheese,
    grated
125 g (4 oz)
    Parmesan cheese,
    grated
salt and pepper

Cook the spinach, with just the
water clinging to the leaves after
washing, until tender. Drain well,
pressing out all excess water. Chop
the spinach.

Heat the oil in a frying pan. Add
the onion and fry until softened. Add
the beef and fry until well browned.
Stir in the mushrooms and fry for a
further 5 minutes. Remove from the
heat and drain off all the fat from the
pan. Add the chopped spinach,
cream, herbs, half the Cheddar and
half the Parmesan. Mix well, adding
salt and pepper to taste, then turn
into a casserole.

Sprinkle the remaining cheeses
over the top. Bake in a preheated
moderate oven, 180°C (350°F), Gas
Mark 4, for 25 minutes.
Serves 4

Lemon Beef Stew

1 tablespoon oil
1 kg (2 lb) beef
  chuck steak, cut
  into cubes
2 large onions,
  chopped
2 lemons, peeled and
  chopped
1 medium green
  pepper, cored,
  seeded and cut in
  rings
1 x 397 g (14 oz)
  can tomatoes
2 teaspoons
  Worcestershire
  sauce
salt and pepper

Pour the oil into a shallow baking dish and add the beef and onions. Put into a preheated hot oven, 230°C (450°F), Gas Mark 8, and cook for 30 minutes or until the beef is browned on all sides, stirring frequently.

Reduce the heat to moderate, 180°C (350°F), Gas Mark 4. Cover the meat with the chopped lemons and green pepper rings. Mix together the tomatoes with their juice, Worcestershire sauce and salt and pepper to taste and pour over the top. Return to the oven and cook for a further 1½ hours or until the meat is tender. If necessary, add a little water to the dish if it seems too dry during the cooking.
Serves 4

Oxtail Casserole

25 g (1 oz) plain
    flour
salt and pepper
2 oxtails, chopped
    into pieces
3 tablespoons brandy
1 onion, chopped
2 carrots, chopped
1 bouquet garni
300 ml (½ pint) red
    wine
    (approximately)
450 ml (¾ pint) beef
    stock or water
    (approximately)

Season the flour and use to coat the oxtail pieces. Place in a casserole and cook in a preheated very hot oven, 230°C (450°F), Gas Mark 8, for 30 minutes, turning frequently.

Pour off all the fat from the casserole. Warm the brandy, pour over the oxtail pieces and set alight. When the flames have died down, add the onion, carrots, bouquet garni, wine and stock or water.

Lower the oven temperature to moderate, 180°C (350°F), Gas Mark 4, and cook for 4 hours or until the oxtail is tender. Stir during cooking and add more liquid as necessary. Discard the bouquet garni.

Serves 4 to 6

Daube de Boeuf

1 large onion, sliced
2 large carrots, sliced
300 ml (½ pint) dry
    white wine
2 cloves garlic, crushed
1 bay leaf
1 teaspoon dried
    thyme
salt and pepper
1.5 kg (3 lb) lean
    chuck steak, cubed
25 g (1 oz) flour
250 g (8 oz) bacon
    rashers, derinded
    and diced
2 teaspoons finely
    chopped orange rind
2 x 397 g (14 oz)
    cans tomatoes,
    drained and chopped
175 g (6 oz)
    mushrooms, sliced
12 black olives
150 ml (¼ pint) stock

Mix together the onion, carrots, wine, garlic, bay leaf, thyme and seasoning in a shallow dish. Add the beef cubes. Leave to marinate in the refrigerator overnight.

Drain the beef, reserving the marinade, and pat dry with kitchen paper. Season the flour and use to coat the beef cubes.

Put about one third of the bacon strips in a flameproof casserole. Spoon over half the marinade, then add half the beef cubes. Sprinkle with half the orange rind, then add half the tomatoes and mushrooms.

Repeat the layers, then top with the black olives and the remaining bacon strips. Pour over the stock.

Bring to the boil on top of the stove, then transfer to a preheated moderate oven, 160°C (325°F), Gas Mark 3, and cook for 4 hours or until tender. Discard the bay leaf.

Serves 6 to 8

Mexican Chilli-Pasta Casserole

2 tablespoons oil
1 medium onion, chopped
500 g (1 lb) minced beef
1 x 397 g (14 oz) can tomatoes
2 tablespoons tomato purée
1 medium green pepper, cored, seeded and diced
1 tablespoon chilli seasoning
salt and pepper
250 g (8 oz) pasta shells
1 x 425 g (15 oz) can red kidney beans, drained
125 g (4 oz) mature Cheddar cheese, grated

Heat the oil in a frying pan, add the onion and fry until softened. Add the beef and brown well, then stir in the tomatoes with their juice, tomato purée, green pepper, chilli seasoning and salt and pepper to taste. Simmer for 15 minutes.

Meanwhile, cook the pasta shells in boiling salted water until tender. Drain well.

Mix the kidney beans into the chilli mixture, then fold in the pasta shells. Turn into a casserole and sprinkle the cheese over the top. Cook in a preheated moderate oven, 180°C (350°F), Gas Mark 4, for 30 minutes.
Serves 4

Gingered Beef

25 g (1 oz) plain
flour
1 teaspoon ground
ginger
salt and pepper
1 kg (2 lb) lean
stewing beef, cut
into 2.5 cm
(1 inch) cubes
3 bacon rashers,
derinded and diced
1 large onion,
chopped
1 clove garlic, crushed
350 g (12 oz)
tomatoes, skinned
and chopped
2 tablespoons tomato
purée
300 ml (½ pint) beef
stock
2 tablespoons soy
sauce
chopped parsley to
garnish

Mix together the flour, ginger and a
little salt and pepper, then use to coat
the beef cubes. Fry the bacon in a
frying pan until it is crisp and has
rendered most of its fat. Remove the
bacon with a slotted spoon and
discard.

Add the beef to the bacon fat in
the pan and fry until browned on all
sides. Transfer to a casserole.

Add the onion and garlic to the
pan and fry until softened. Stir in the
tomatoes, tomato purée, beef stock,
soy sauce and salt and pepper to
taste. Pour into the casserole, cover
and cook in a preheated moderate
oven, 180°C (350°F), Gas Mark 4, for
2½ to 3 hours or until the beef is
tender. Garnish with chopped
parsley.
Serves 4

Illustrated above:
Gingered beef;
Beef casseroled with
horseradish (page 28).

27

Beef Casseroled with Horseradish

25 g (1 oz) plain
 flour
salt and pepper
1-1.25 kg (2-2½ lb)
 piece of beef top
 rump
25 g (1 oz) beef
 dripping
6 tablespoons
 horseradish sauce
250 ml (8 fl oz)
 water
4 small potatoes,
 halved
4 medium carrots,
 sliced
4 button onions

Season the flour and use to coat the beef. Melt the dripping in a flameproof casserole, add the beef and brown on all sides. Spread the horseradish sauce all over the beef and pour in the water. Cover tightly and cook in a preheated moderate oven, 160°C (325°F), Gas Mark 3, for 2½ hours.

Add the vegetables to the casserole with salt and pepper to taste. Re-cover the casserole and cook for a further 1 hour or until the meat and vegetables are tender.
Serves 4

Illustrated on page 27.

Boeuf Stroganof en Casserole

25 g (1 oz) butter
1 kg (2 lb) lean
 stewing beef, cut
 into strips
1 tablespoon oil
1 onion, sliced
250 g (8 oz)
 mushrooms, sliced
2 tablespoons plain
 flour
150 ml (¼ pint) beef
 stock
150 ml (¼ pint)
 fresh sour cream
1 ½ tablespoons
 tomato purée
salt and pepper
chopped parsley to
 garnish

Melt the butter in a frying pan, add the beef strips and fry, turning, until evenly browned. Remove the beef strips from the pan with a slotted spoon and place in a casserole.

Add the oil to the frying pan and heat, then add the onion and mushrooms and fry until the onion is softened. Sprinkle over the flour and cook, stirring, for 2 minutes. Gradually stir in the stock. Remove from the heat and stir in the cream, tomato purée and salt and pepper to taste. Pour this mixture into the casserole and stir well.

Cover tightly and cook in a preheated moderate oven, 160°C (325°F), Gas Mark 3, for 1 hour or until the beef is tender. Garnish with chopped parsley.
Serves 4

Beef Carbonnade

50 g (2 oz) beef
 dripping
1 kg (2 lb) chuck
 steak, cubed
2 onions, sliced
15 g (½ oz) plain
 flour
300 ml (½ pint)
 stout
300 ml (½ pint)
 stock or water
salt and pepper
1 bouquet garni
pinch of grated
 nutmeg
pinch of sugar
1½ teaspoons wine
 vinegar

Melt the dripping in a flameproof casserole. Add the steak cubes, in batches, and brown on all sides. Remove from the casserole.

Add the onions to the casserole and fry until golden brown. Sprinkle over the flour and cook, stirring, for 2 minutes. Gradually stir in the stout and stock or water and bring to the boil. Add salt and pepper to taste, the bouquet garni, nutmeg, sugar and vinegar. Return the meat to the casserole and stir well.

Cover tightly and cook in a preheated moderate oven, 160°C (325°F), Gas Mark 3, for 2 hours or until the meat is tender. Discard the bouquet garni before serving.

Serves 4

VEAL

Braised Sweetbreads

500 g (1 lb) calf's
  sweetbreads
25 g (1 oz) butter
1 medium onion,
  finely chopped
1 large carrot, finely
  chopped
1 celery stick, finely
  chopped
4 slices cooked ham,
  cut into strips
150 ml (1/4 pint)
  stock
150 ml (1/4 pint) dry
  white wine
salt and pepper

Blanch the sweetbreads in boiling
water for 5 minutes. Drain, then
remove ducts and skin and slice.

Melt the butter in a flameproof
casserole. Add the onion, carrot,
celery and ham and cook until the
onion is softened. Stir in the stock,
wine and salt and pepper to taste and
bring to the boil. Arrange the
sweetbreads on top of the vegetables,
cover and cook in a preheated
moderately hot oven, 190°C (375°F),
Gas Mark 5, for 30 minutes.
Serves 4

Golden-Top Casserole

500 g (1 lb) boned
  veal shoulder or
  pie veal, cubed
500 g (1 lb) boned
  pork chump
  (escalope), cubed
stock or water
250 g (8 oz) noodles
salt and pepper
1 x 298 g (10½ oz)
  can condensed
  cream of chicken
  soup
350 g (12 oz)
  Cheddar cheese,
  grated
1 x 326 g (11½ oz)
  can sweetcorn,
  drained
50 g (2 oz) fresh
  breadcrumbs

Put the veal and pork in a saucepan, add stock or water to cover and bring to the boil, skimming off the scum that rises to the surface. Simmer for 45 minutes.

Meanwhile, cook the noodles in boiling salted water until tender. Drain and mix with the soup, 250 g (8 oz) of the cheese and salt and pepper to taste.

Drain the veal and pork and add to the noodle mixture. Stir well and turn into a casserole.

Spread the sweetcorn over the meat and noodle mixture. Combine the breadcrumbs with the remaining cheese and scatter over the top. Cook in a preheated moderate oven, 180°C (350°F), Gas Mark 4, for 20 to 30 minutes or until the top is browned.
Serves 4

Braised sweetbreads;
Veal goulash (page 32);
Golden-top casserole.

Veal Goulash

40 g (1½ oz) butter
2 streaky bacon
    rashers, derinded
    and diced
1 medium onion,
    chopped
125 g (4 oz)
    mushrooms, sliced
1 kg (2 lb) boned
    veal shoulder,
    cubed
½ teaspoon paprika
300 ml (½ pint)
    fresh sour cream
150 ml (¼ pint) beef
    stock or water
salt and pepper
paprika to garnish

Melt the butter in a frying pan, add the bacon and onion and fry until golden. Stir in the mushrooms and fry for a further 5 minutes. Transfer with a slotted spoon to a casserole.

Add the veal to the frying pan and brown on all sides. As the veal cubes brown, transfer to the casserole.

Sprinkle the paprika into the fat remaining in the frying pan and cook, stirring, for 2 minutes. Stir in the sour cream, stock or water and salt and pepper to taste. Pour into the casserole and stir well. Cover the casserole and cook in a preheated moderate oven, 160°C (325°F), Gas Mark 3, for 1 hour or until tender. Sprinkle with paprika to garnish.
Serves 4

Illustrated on page 30.

Veal Parmesan

25 g (1 oz) dry
    breadcrumbs
25 g (1 oz) grated
    Parmesan cheese
salt and pepper
500 g (1 lb) veal
    escalopes, cut into
    squares
1 egg, beaten
40 g (1½ oz) butter,
    melted
2 tablespoons olive oil
1 onion, thinly sliced
500 g (1 lb)
    tomatoes, skinned
    and chopped
2 tablespoons tomato
    purée
½ teaspoon sugar
½ teaspoon dried
    oregano
chopped parsley to
    garnish

Mix together the breadcrumbs, cheese and salt and pepper to taste. Dip the veal into the beaten egg, then coat with the cheese mixture.

Pour the melted butter into a baking dish and arrange the veal squares in the dish, in one layer, turning them to coat with the melted butter. Cook in a preheated moderately hot oven, 200°C (400°F), Gas Mark 6, for 20 minutes. Turn the veal and cook for 15 minutes.

Meanwhile, heat the oil in a saucepan and fry the onion until softened. Add the tomatoes, tomato purée, sugar, oregano and salt and pepper to taste and stir well. Simmer until the sauce is well reduced.

Pour the tomato sauce over the veal and heat through in the oven for 5 to 10 minutes before serving, garnished with chopped parsley.
Serves 4

Veal with Orange

25 g (1 oz) butter
1 tablespoon oil
750 g (1½ lb) pie
veal, cubed
1 onion, sliced
3 tablespoons plain
flour
300 ml (½ pint)
chicken stock
150 ml (¼ pint)
orange juice
salt and pepper
2 oranges, peeled and
sliced
watercress to garnish

Melt the butter with the oil in a
frying pan. Add the veal cubes and
brown on all sides. Transfer with a
slotted spoon to a casserole.

Add the onion to the pan and fry
until golden brown. Add to the
casserole.

Stir the flour into the fat
remaining in the pan and cook for 3
minutes. Gradually stir in the stock
and orange juice and bring to the
boil. Season with salt and pepper to
taste. Pour over the veal cubes.
Arrange the orange slices,
overlapping, on top.

Cook in a preheated moderate
oven, 180°C (350°F), Gas Mark 4, for
1½ to 2 hours or until the veal is
tender. Garnish with watercress.
Serves 4

Meatball Casserole

1 kg (2 lb) minced
   veal
4 tablespoons fresh
   breadcrumbs
2 tablespoons grated
   Parmesan cheese
2 tablespoons
   chopped parsley
salt and pepper
1 small egg, beaten
25 g (1 oz) butter
1 tablespoon oil
1 onion, chopped
2 celery sticks,
   chopped
1 apple, peeled,
   cored and diced
150 ml (¼ pint) stock
150 ml (¼ pint) red
   wine
4 tablespoons sweet
   pickle
2 tablespoons
   chopped sultanas
chopped parsley to
   garnish

Mix together the veal, breadcrumbs, cheese, parsley and salt and pepper to taste. Bind the mixture with the egg. Shape into meatballs about the size of walnuts.

Melt the butter with the oil in a frying pan. Add the meatballs, in batches, and brown on all sides, then transfer to a casserole.

Add the onion, celery and apple to the frying pan and fry until the onion is softened. Stir in the stock, wine, pickle and sultanas and bring to the boil. Simmer for 10 minutes.

Pour the sauce over the meatballs. Cover and cook in a preheated moderately hot oven, 190°C (375°F), Gas Mark 5, for 30 minutes or until the meatballs are cooked through. Garnish with chopped parsley.
Serves 4

Roman Veal Casserole

25 g (1 oz) plain
    flour
salt and pepper
1 kg (2 lb) veal
    escalopes, cut into
    squares
25 g (1 oz) butter
1 tablespoon olive oil
250 g (8 oz)
    mushrooms, sliced
1 clove garlic, crushed
1 x 397 g (14 oz)
    can tomatoes,
    drained and
    chopped
150 ml (¼ pint)
    Marsala
1 teaspoon dried basil
½ teaspoon dried
    oregano
chopped parsley to
    garnish

Season the flour and use to coat the veal squares. Melt the butter with the oil in a flameproof casserole. Add the veal and brown on all sides, then remove and set aside.

Add the mushrooms and garlic to the casserole and fry for 3 minutes. Stir in the tomatoes, Marsala, herbs and seasoning to taste. Bring to the boil.

Return the veal to the casserole and mix into the sauce. Cover and cook in a preheated moderate oven, 160°C (325°F), Gas Mark 3, for 45 minutes. Serve garnished with parsley.
Serves 4

LAMB

Irish Stew

50 g (2 oz) butter
8 lamb chops
1 large onion,
    chopped
1 tablespoon plain
    flour
1 x 411 g (14½ oz)
    can consommé
1 bouquet garni
salt and pepper
1 kg (2 lb) potatoes,
    cut into 4 cm (1½
    inch) chunks
chopped parsley to
    garnish

Melt the butter in a flameproof casserole. Add the chops and brown on both sides, then remove and set aside. Add the onion to the casserole and fry until softened. Sprinkle over the flour and stir well, then return the chops to the casserole.

Pour over the consommé and add the bouquet garni with salt and pepper to taste. Bring to the boil, then cover and cook in a preheated moderate oven, 180°C (350°F), Gas Mark 4, for 1 hour.

Stir in the potatoes, re-cover the casserole and continue cooking for 45 minutes or until the chops are cooked and the potatoes tender. Remove the bouquet garni. Garnish with parsley before serving.
Serves 4

*Irish stew; Kidney ragoût;
Lamb ratatouille
(page 38).*

Kidney Ragoût

3 tablespoons plain
    flour
salt and pepper
25 g (1 oz) butter
250 g (8 oz)
    unsmoked streaky
    bacon rashers,
    derinded and diced
12 lambs' kidneys,
    sliced
1 large onion, finely
    chopped
1 clove garlic, crushed
1 red pepper, cored,
    seeded and diced
2 tomatoes, skinned,
    seeded and
    chopped
150 ml (¼ pint) beef
    stock
6 tablespoons red wine
triangles of fried
    bread to garnish

Season the flour and use to coat the kidney slices. Melt the butter in a frying pan and fry the bacon until crisp. Remove with a slotted spoon and place in a casserole.

Add the kidney slices to the frying pan and brown on all sides. Transfer to the casserole.

Add the onion, garlic and red pepper to the frying pan and fry until the onion is softened. Stir in the tomatoes, stock and wine and bring to the boil, then pour into the casserole and mix well. Cover and cook in a preheated moderate oven, 180°C (350°F), Gas Mark 4, for 30 minutes or until the kidneys are tender. Garnish with triangles of fried bread before serving.
Serves 4

Lamb Ratatouille

1 large aubergine,
    halved lengthways
    and sliced
salt and pepper
4 tablespoons olive
    oil
    (approximately)
1 kg (2 lb) boned
    shoulder of lamb,
    cubed
1 large onion, sliced
750 g (1½ lb)
    courgettes, sliced
½ red and ½ green
    pepper, cored,
    seeded and sliced
1 x 397 g (14 oz)
    can tomatoes
1 teaspoon dried basil

Sprinkle the aubergine slices with salt and leave to drain for 30 minutes. Rinse and pat dry.

Heat 3 tablespoons of the oil in a flameproof casserole. Add the lamb cubes and brown on all sides, then remove and set aside.

Add the onion to the casserole, with the remaining oil if necessary, and fry until softened. Add the aubergine, courgettes, red or green pepper, tomatoes with their juice, basil and salt and pepper to taste. Cover and cook for 10 minutes.

Stir the lamb cubes into the vegetable mixture. Re-cover and cook in a preheated moderate oven, 180°C (350°F), Gas Mark 4, for 1 hour or until tender.

Serves 4 to 6

Illustrated on page 37.

Orange Lamb Casserole

1 large onion, sliced
2 teaspoons dried
    marjoram
1 orange
1.75 kg (4 lb) loin of
    lamb, in one piece
salt and pepper
300 ml (½ pint) dry
    white wine or
    stock
150 ml (¼ pint)
    orange juice
1 tablespoon orange
    marmalade

Put the onion slices in a greased casserole and sprinkle with the marjoram. Pare the rind from the orange in strips and scatter over the onion. Peel and slice the orange.

Rub the lamb with salt and pepper and place in the casserole. Arrange the orange slices over the meat. Pour in the wine or stock and orange juice.

Cover and cook in a preheated moderate oven, 160°C (325°F), Gas Mark 3, for 2 to 2½ hours or until the meat is tender.

Transfer the meat to a warmed serving dish. Arrange the orange slices on top and keep hot.

Strain the cooking liquid into a saucepan. Skim off the fat and boil until reduced and thickened. Stir in the marmalade and adjust the seasoning. Serve with the lamb.

Serves 4

Moussaka

2 medium
  aubergines, sliced
salt and pepper
6 tablespoons olive
  oil
  (approximately)
1 large onion,
  chopped
1 clove garlic, finely
  chopped
750 g (1 ½ lb)
  cooked lamb,
  finely chopped
250 g (8 oz)
  tomatoes, skinned
  and chopped
2 tablespoons
  chopped parsley
grated nutmeg
25 g (1 oz) butter
25 g (1 oz) plain
  flour
300 ml (½ pint)
  milk
1 egg yolk
parsley sprigs to
  garnish

Sprinkle the aubergine slices with salt and leave to drain for 30 minutes. Rinse and pat dry with kitchen paper. Heat a little of the olive oil in a frying pan. Fry the aubergine slices, in batches, until golden brown on both sides, adding more oil as necessary.

Add the onion and garlic to the pan, with more oil if necessary, and fry until softened. Stir in the lamb, tomatoes, parsley, salt, pepper and nutmeg to taste. Cook for 5 minutes.

Make alternate layers of aubergine and lamb in a casserole, beginning and ending with aubergine slices.

Melt the butter in a saucepan. Add the flour and cook, stirring, for 1 minute. Gradually stir in the milk and bring to the boil. Simmer, stirring, until thickened. Season with salt, pepper and nutmeg to taste. Cool slightly, then beat in the egg yolk.

Pour the sauce over the aubergine slices. Cook in a preheated moderate oven, 180°C (350°F), Gas Mark 4, for 45 minutes. Garnish with parsley.

Serves 4

Liver and Bacon Hotpot

1 large onion, sliced
2 medium cooking
  apples, peeled,
  cored and sliced
125 g (4 oz)
  mushrooms, sliced
250 (8 oz)
  unsmoked back
  bacon rashers,
  derinded
750 g (1½ lb)
  lamb's liver, sliced
salt and pepper
½ x 411 g (14½ oz)
  can consommé
1 x 397 g (14 oz)
  can tomatoes,
  drained and
  chopped
chopped parsley to
  garnish

Spread one third of the onion over the bottom of a greased casserole. Add one third of the apple slices, then one third of the mushrooms and bacon, then half the liver. Season well. Continue making layers in this way. Pour in the consommé and spread the tomatoes over the top. Cover tightly and cook in a preheated moderate oven, 180°C (350°F), Gas Mark 4, for 1½ hours. Serve garnished with chopped parsley.
Serves 4

Somerset Lamb Chops

25 g (1 oz) butter
1 tablespoon oil
1 large onion, thinly
  sliced
2 large cooking
  apples, peeled,
  cored and sliced
2 tablespoons raisins
2 tablespoons brown
  sugar
salt and pepper
8 or 12 lamb chops
150 ml (¼ pint) dry
  cider

Melt the butter with the oil in a
frying pan. Add the onion and fry
until softened. Remove the onion
from the pan with a slotted spoon
and spread half over the bottom of a
casserole. Cover with half the apple
slices and sprinkle with half the
raisins, half the sugar and salt and
pepper to taste.

Put the chops in the frying pan
and brown on both sides. Drain the
chops and place in the casserole.
Cover with the rest of the onion and
apples and sprinkle with the
remaining raisins, sugar, salt and
pepper. Pour in the cider.

Cover the casserole and cook in a
preheated moderate oven, 180°C
(350°F), Gas Mark 4, for 1½ hours or
until the chops are very tender.
Serves 4

Lamb, Pork and Potato Casserole

25 g (1 oz) butter
750 g (1 ½ lb)
   potatoes, sliced
500 g (1 lb) boned
   shoulder of lamb,
   cubed
500 g (1 lb) boned
   shoulder of pork,
   cubed
2 onions, chopped
salt and pepper
150 ml (¼ pint) dry
   white wine

Grease a casserole with half the butter. Make a layer of half the potato slices on the bottom, then add the lamb, pork and onions in layers, sprinkling each layer with a little salt and pepper. Pour over the wine. Arrange the remaining potato slices on top and dot with the remaining butter. Cover and cook in a preheated moderately hot oven, 190°C (375°F), Gas Mark 5, for 1½ hours.

Uncover the casserole and continue cooking for 30 minutes or until the potato topping is golden brown.
Serves 4

Lamb with Mushrooms and Tomatoes

40 g (1½ oz) butter
250 g (8 oz)
  mushrooms,
  chopped
15 g (½ oz) flour
150 ml (¼ pint) milk
150 ml (¼ pint)
  chicken stock
2 tablespoons
  medium sherry
salt and pepper
750 g (1½ lb)
  cooked lamb,
  chopped
500 g (1 lb) tomatoes,
  skinned and sliced
25 g (1 oz) fresh
  breadcrumbs
25 g (1 oz) mature
  Cheddar cheese,
  grated
2 tablespoons
  chopped parsley

Melt the butter in a saucepan. Add the mushrooms and fry for 3 minutes. Sprinkle over the flour and cook, stirring, for 2 minutes. Gradually stir in the milk and stock. Bring to the boil and simmer, stirring, until thickened. Add the sherry and salt and pepper to taste, then fold in the lamb. Turn into a greased baking dish.

Arrange the tomato slices over the lamb mixture. Combine the breadcrumbs, cheese and parsley and sprinkle over the top. Bake in a preheated moderate oven, 180°C (350°F), Gas Mark 4, for 30 minutes or until the top is golden brown.
Serves 4

Haricot of Lamb

350 g (12 oz) dried
  white haricot
  beans, soaked
  overnight
1 onion, stuck with 4
  cloves
1 bay leaf
salt and pepper
3 tablespoons plain
  flour
1 kg (2 lb) boned
  lamb shoulder, cut
  into 2.5 cm
  (1 inch) cubes
3 tablespoons oil
2 cloves garlic, finely
  chopped
1 large onion,
  chopped
1 x 397 g (14 oz)
  can tomatoes,
  drained
450 ml (¾ pint)
  chicken stock
  (approximately)
1 tablespoon lemon
  juice
1 teaspoon dried
  thyme
25 g (1 oz) dry
  breadcrumbs
15 g (½ oz) butter,
  melted

Drain the beans and put them in a saucepan with the onion stuck with cloves, the bay leaf and 1 teaspoon salt. Pour over water to cover and bring to the boil. Simmer gently for 1 hour or until the beans are tender.

Meanwhile, season the flour and use to coat the lamb cubes. Heat the oil in a flameproof casserole, add the garlic and chopped onion and fry until softened. Add the lamb cubes and brown on all sides. Stir in the tomatoes, stock, lemon juice and thyme and bring to the boil. Cover and cook in a preheated moderate oven, 180°C (350°F), Gas Mark 4, for 1 hour.

Drain the beans, discarding the onion and bay leaf, and add to the casserole. Stir well. Add a little more stock if necessary. Re-cover the casserole and cook for a further 1 hour or until the lamb is tender.

Mix together the breadcrumbs and butter. Uncover the casserole and sprinkle over the breadcrumbs. Cook for 15 to 20 minutes or until the topping is golden brown.
Serves 4 to 6

PORK

Plummy Pork Chops

15 g (½ oz) butter
1 tablespoon oil
4 or 8 pork chops
500 g (1 lb) plums,
  stoned
sugar
½ teaspoon ground
  allspice
3 tablespoons water
150 ml (¼ pint) red
  wine
  (approximately)
salt and pepper
watercress to garnish

Melt the butter with the oil in a frying pan. Add the chops and brown on both sides, then drain and place in a shallow casserole.

Put the plums, sugar to taste, allspice and water in a saucepan and cook gently until the plums are very soft. Allow to cool slightly, then rub through a sieve or purée in an electric blender. Mix in the red wine and salt and pepper to taste, then pour over the chops. Add more red wine if necessary so the chops are just covered.

Cover and cook in a preheated moderate oven, 180°C (350°F), Gas Mark 4, for 45 minutes or until the chops are tender. Serve garnished with watercress.
Serves 4

Plummy pork chops; Pork and French beans; Pork in mushroom sauce (page 48).

Pork and French Beans

3 tablespoons plain
  flour
1/2 teaspoon ground
  ginger
salt and pepper
1 kg (2 lb) boned
  pork shoulder,
  trimmed of fat and
  cut into cubes
25 g (1 oz) butter
2 tablespoons oil
2 onions, thinly
  sliced
1 clove garlic,
  crushed
450 ml (3/4 pint)
  chicken stock
  (approximately)
250 g (8 oz)
  tomatoes, skinned
  and chopped
350 g (12 oz)
  French beans, cut
  into 5 cm (2 inch)
  lengths

Mix the flour with the ginger and a little salt and pepper, then use to coat the pork cubes. Melt the butter with the oil in a flameproof casserole. Add the onions and garlic and fry until softened. Add the pork cubes and brown on all sides. Stir in enough stock to cover the pork and bring to the boil. Cover the casserole and cook in a preheated moderate oven, 160°C (325°F), Gas Mark 3, for 2½ hours.

Skim any fat from the surface, then stir in the tomatoes. Lay the beans over the top and press down gently so they become moistened with the cooking liquid. Re–cover the casserole and continue cooking for a further 30 minutes.

Serves 4

Pork in Mushroom Sauce

50 g (2 oz) butter
2 tablespoons oil
1 kg (2 lb) pork
  fillet, sliced
1 large onion, sliced
salt and pepper
300 ml (½ pint) dry
  red wine
250 g (8 oz)
  mushrooms, sliced
15 g (½ oz) plain
  flour
300 ml (½ pint)
  double cream
chopped chives to
  garnish

Melt the butter with the oil in a frying pan. Add the pork slices and brown on both sides. Remove from the pan with a slotted spoon and place in a flameproof casserole.

Add the onion to the frying pan and fry until softened. Drain and arrange over the pork. Add salt and pepper to taste, and the wine.

Cover and cook in a preheated moderate oven, 180°C (350°F), Gas Mark 4, for 1¼ hours. Stir in the mushrooms and cook for 15 minutes or until the pork is tender.

Mix together the flour and cream and stir into the casserole. Cook gently on top of the stove, stirring, until the liquid has thickened; do not boil. Serve garnished with chives.
Serves 4

Illustrated on page 47.

Barbecued Sparerib Casserole

8 pork sparerib chops
salt and pepper
25 g (1 oz) butter
1 tablespoon oil
1 onion, chopped
1 clove garlic, crushed
250 ml (8 fl oz)
  tomato ketchup
450 ml (¾ pint)
  water
4 tablespoons cider
  vinegar
4 tablespoons
  Worcestershire
  sauce
40 g (1½ oz) brown
  sugar
1 teaspoon mild chilli
  powder
few drops of Tabasco
  sauce
8 lemon slices

Rub the chops with salt and pepper on both sides. Melt the butter with the oil in a frying pan. Add the chops, in batches, and brown on both sides, then transfer to a baking dish, arranging them in one layer if possible.

Add the onion and garlic to the frying pan and fry until softened. Stir in the ketchup, water, vinegar, Worcestershire sauce, brown sugar, chilli powder and Tabasco sauce and bring to the boil. Simmer for 30 minutes.

Taste the sauce and adjust the seasoning. Place a lemon slice on each pork chop, then pour over the sauce. Bake in a preheated moderate oven, 180°C (350°F), Gas Mark 4, for 1½ hours or until the chops are tender, turning them occasionally.
Serves 4

Chilli Pork

2 tablespoons oil
1 large onion,
  chopped
1 green pepper,
  cored, seeded and
  diced
1 kg (2 lb) pork
  chump (escalope),
  cubed
1 x 298 g (10½ oz)
  can condensed
  tomato soup
2 celery sticks, chopped
1 tablespoon chilli
  seasoning
1 x 397 g (14 oz)
  can tomatoes,
  drained and
  chopped
1 x 425 g (15 oz)
  can red kidney
  beans, drained
salt and pepper

Heat the oil in a flameproof
casserole. Add the onion and green
pepper and fry until softened. Stir in
the pork cubes and brown lightly on
all sides. Cover tightly and cook in a
preheated moderate oven, 180°C
(350°F), Gas Mark 4, for 40 minutes.

Stir in the soup, celery, chilli
seasoning and tomatoes. Re-cover
the casserole and cook for a further
20 minutes or until the pork is
tender. Stir in the kidney beans with
salt and pepper to taste. Cook,
uncovered, for a further 10 minutes
or until the beans are heated through.
Serves 4

Sausage and Bean Casserole

*500 g (1 lb) pork
  sausages
1 large onion,
  chopped
2 x 446 g (15³/4 oz)
  cans baked beans
175 g (6 oz) dried
  apricots, finely
  chopped
2 tablespoons brown
  sugar
1 teaspoon dry
  mustard
salt and pepper*

Prick the sausages all over, then fry in a dry frying pan until they are browned all over and have rendered some of their fat. Remove from the pan, cut into 1 cm (¹/2 inch) slices and set aside.

Pour off all but 2 tablespoons fat from the pan and add the onion. Fry until softened then drain and put into a casserole. Add the sausage slices, baked beans, apricots, sugar and mustard. Mix well and add salt and pepper to taste. Cover and cook in a preheated moderate oven, 180°C (350°F), Gas Mark 4, for 30 to 45 minutes or until heated through.
Serves 4

Cidered Sausages

15 g (½ oz) butter
3 bacon rashers, de-
   rinded and diced
500 g (1 lb) pork
   sausages
2 onions, sliced
1 large carrot, diced
1 green pepper, cored,
   seeded and diced
3 tablespoons flour
350 ml (12 fl oz)
   dry cider
1 tablespoon Worces-
   tershire sauce
salt and pepper
TOPPING:
65 g (2½ oz) corn
   meal
50 g (2 oz) plain
   flour
2 teaspoons baking
   powder
pinch of sugar
¼ teaspoon salt
1 large egg
25 g (1 oz)
   margarine, melted
7 tablespoons milk
   (approximately)

Melt the butter in a frying pan, add the bacon and fry until crisp. Remove with a slotted spoon.

Add the sausages to the pan and brown on all sides, then remove from the pan and cut in half.

Add the onions, carrot and green pepper to the pan and fry until the onions are softened. Sprinkle over the flour and cook, stirring, for 2 minutes. Gradually stir in the cider and Worcestershire sauce and bring to the boil, stirring. Season with salt and pepper to taste.

Return the bacon and sausages to the pan and stir well. Cover and simmer while making the topping.

Mix together the corn meal, flour, baking powder, sugar and salt. Add the egg, margarine and enough milk to make a smooth thick batter.

Pour the sausage mixture into a deep baking dish not more than 20 cm (8 inches) in diameter. Pour the cornbread topping over. Cook in a preheated hot oven, 225°C (425°F), Gas Mark 7, for 15 to 20 minutes.
Serves 4

Ham and Egg Pie

4 medium potatoes
salt and pepper
250 g (8 oz) cooked
   ham, chopped
6 hard-boiled eggs,
   sliced
125 g (4 oz)
   Cheddar cheese,
   grated
4 spring onions,
   chopped
300 ml (½ pint)
   fresh sour cream
2 tomatoes, sliced
chopped chives to
   garnish

Cook the potatoes in boiling, salted water until tender. Drain and slice.

Make alternate layers of potato, ham, eggs and cheese in a greased casserole, sprinkling each layer of egg slices with salt and pepper and chopped spring onions. Begin and end with potato slices. Pour the cream over the top and arrange the tomato slices in a ring around the edge. Bake in a preheated moderate oven, 180°C (350°F), Gas Mark 4, for 30 minutes. Serve garnished with chives.
Serves 4

Somerset Pork Casserole

25 g (1 oz) butter
2 large cooking
    apples, peeled,
    cored and sliced
1 large onion,
    chopped
2 teaspoons sugar
2 teaspoons dried
    sage
4 or 8 pork chops
salt and pepper
125 g (4 oz)
    mushrooms, sliced
150 ml (¼ pint) dry
    cider
50 g (2 oz) fresh
    breadcrumbs
50 g (2 oz) mature
    Cheddar cheese,
    grated

Grease a shallow baking dish with half the butter. Place half the apple slices in the dish and sprinkle with half the onion, sugar and sage. Arrange the chops on top, season with salt and pepper to taste and cover with the mushrooms. Add the remaining apples, onion, sugar and sage. Pour in the cider.

Mix together the breadcrumbs and cheese and sprinkle over the top. Dot with the remaining butter. Cook in a preheated moderately hot oven, 200°C (400°F), Gas Mark 6, for 45 minutes or until the chops are cooked and the top is browned.
Serves 4

Pork Casseroled with Fruit

15 g (½ oz) butter
1 tablespoon oil
4 or 8 pork chops
1 x 411 g (14½ oz)
  can apricot halves
1 x 227 g (8 oz) can
  pineapple rings
8 prunes, stoned and
  chopped
25 g (1 oz) brown
  sugar
5 tablespoons chicken
  stock
150 ml (¼ pint)
  single cream
salt and pepper

Melt the butter with the oil in a frying pan. Add the chops and brown on both sides. Remove the chops from the pan, drain, then arrange in a flameproof casserole.

Drain the apricot halves and pineapple rings, reserving the syrup. Place the fruit, with the prunes, on top of the chops to cover them. Sprinkle with the brown sugar.

Mix the stock with 5 tablespoons each of the apricot and pineapple syrups. Pour into the casserole.

Cover tightly and cook in a preheated moderate oven, 180°C (350°F), Gas Mark 4, for about 1 hour or until the chops are tender.

Transfer the chops to a warmed serving dish, being careful not to dislodge the fruit on top. Keep hot.

Boil the liquid in the casserole until reduced to about 150 ml (¼ pint). Skim off any fat, then stir in the cream with salt and pepper to taste. Heat through gently and serve this sauce with the pork.
Serves 4

POULTRY & GAME

Casseroled Grouse

2 oven-ready grouse
salt and pepper
50 g (2 oz) butter
1 onion, chopped
2 carrots, diced
1 celery stick,
    chopped
300 ml (½ pint)
    stock
150 ml (¼ pint) red
    wine
1 bay leaf
2 tablespoons
    redcurrant jelly
parsley sprigs to
    garnish

Rub the grouse with seasoning. Melt the butter in a flameproof casserole, add the grouse and brown on all sides, then remove and set aside.

Add the onion, carrots and celery to the casserole and fry until softened. Stir in the stock, wine and bay leaf and bring to the boil. Return the grouse to the casserole.

Cover and cook in a preheated moderate oven, 180°C (350°F), Gas Mark 4, for 1¼ hours or until the grouse are tender. Transfer the grouse to a warmed serving dish and keep hot. Skim any fat from the cooking liquid, then rub through a sieve or purée in an electric blender. Return to the casserole and boil until well reduced and thickened. Adjust the seasoning and stir in the redcurrant jelly. Serve with the grouse. Garnish the dish with parsley.
Serves 4

Duckling and Orange Casserole

1 x 2.5 kg (5 lb) duckling, quartered and skinned
25 g (1 oz) butter
1 small onion, finely chopped
150 ml (¼ pint) orange juice
¼ teaspoon dried tarragon
pinch of dry mustard
2 tablespoons port
4 tablespoons redcurrant jelly
1 orange
salt and pepper
2 teaspoons cornflour

Remove all fat from the duckling quarters, then place them in a flameproof casserole.

Melt the butter in a saucepan, add the onion and fry until softened. Stir in all but 1 tablespoon of the orange juice, the tarragon, mustard, port and redcurrant jelly. Grate the rind from the orange and add to the pan with salt and pepper to taste. Bring to the boil, stirring, then pour over the duckling quarters.

Peel the orange, divide into segments and place on top of the duckling. Cover and cook in a preheated moderate oven, 180°C (350°F), Gas Mark 4, for 1 hour or until the duckling is tender. Transfer the duckling quarters and orange segments to a serving dish and keep hot.

Skim any fat from the surface of the cooking liquid. Dissolve the cornflour in the reserved orange juice and stir into the cooking liquid. Simmer on top of the stove, stirring, until thickened. Serve with the duckling.
Serves 4

Casseroled grouse; Duckling and orange casserole; Turkey bake (page 56).

Turkey Bake

350 g (12 oz) cooked
 turkey, chopped
2 medium potatoes,
 cooked and diced
1 onion, grated
150 ml (¼ pint)
 milk
1 small egg, beaten
1 teaspoon grated
 lemon rind
salt and pepper
8 water biscuits,
 finely crushed
15 g (½ oz) butter,
 melted

Mix together the turkey, potatoes, onion, milk, egg, lemon rind and salt and pepper to taste. Turn into a greased casserole.

Combine the crushed biscuits and melted butter and sprinkle over the top. Cook in a preheated moderate oven, 180°C (350°F), Gas Mark 4, for about 30 minutes.

Serves 4

Illustrated on page 55.

Rabbit in Cranberry Sauce

4 rabbit quarters
1 tablespoon vinegar
25 g (1 oz) plain
 flour
salt and pepper
¼ teaspoon ground
 allspice
25 g (1 oz) butter
2 tablespoons oil
1 onion, chopped
1 large carrot, diced
300 ml (½ pint)
 chicken stock
300 ml (½ pint) dry
 white wine
1 bay leaf
125 g (4 oz) canned
 whole berry
 cranberry sauce

Soak the rabbit quarters overnight in water with the vinegar added. Drain, rinse and pat dry with kitchen paper.

Season the flour with salt and pepper and the allspice and use to coat the rabbit quarters. Melt the butter with the oil in a flameproof casserole. Add the rabbit quarters and brown on all sides, then remove.

Add the onion and carrot to the casserole and fry until softened. Stir in the stock and wine and bring to the boil. Return the rabbit quarters to the casserole with the bay leaf. Cover and cook in a preheated moderate oven, 180°C (350°F), Gas Mark 4, for 1½ hours or until tender.

Remove the rabbit pieces from the casserole and keep warm. Boil the cooking liquid until reduced to about 300 ml (½ pint). Strain the liquid and return to the casserole. Stir in the cranberry sauce and adjust seasoning.

Return the rabbit to the casserole and turn to coat with the sauce. Cover and return to the oven for 10 minutes or until heated through.

Serves 4

Rabbit with Mustard Sauce

4 rabbit quarters
1 tablespoon vinegar
25 g (1 oz) butter
250 g (8 oz)
  unsmoked streaky
  bacon, derinded
  and diced
2 onions, chopped
15 g (½ oz) plain
  flour
450 ml (¾ pint)
  chicken stock
salt and pepper
1 bouquet garni
150 ml (¼ pint)
  double cream
2 tablespoons French
  mustard
chopped parsley to
  garnish

Soak the rabbit quarters overnight in water with the vinegar added. Drain, rinse and pat dry with kitchen paper.

Melt the butter in a flameproof casserole. Add the rabbit quarters and brown on all sides, then remove.

Add the bacon and onions to the casserole and fry until golden brown. Sprinkle over the flour and cook, stirring, for 2 minutes. Gradually stir in the stock and bring to the boil. Season with salt and pepper to taste, then return the rabbit to the casserole and add the bouquet garni.

Cover and cook in a preheated moderate oven, 180°C (350°F), Gas Mark 4, for 1½ hours or until tender.

Remove the rabbit from the casserole. Discard the bouquet garni. Mix the cream with the mustard and stir into the cooking liquid. Heat, stirring, on top of the stove; do not boil. Return the rabbit and reheat. Serve garnished with parsley.
Serves 4

Hunter's Casserole

300 ml (½ pint) dry
    red wine
4 tablespoons olive
    oil
1 clove garlic,
    crushed
1 bay leaf
salt and pepper
1 kg (2 lb) boneless
    hare, cut into
    cubes
25 g (1 oz) butter
2 large carrots, sliced
150 ml (¼ pint) beef
    stock
250 g (8 oz) baby
    onions
250 g (8 oz) button
    mushrooms

Mix together the wine, oil, garlic,
bay leaf and salt and pepper in a
shallow dish. Add the hare and leave
to marinate overnight, turning
occasionally.

Drain the hare, reserving the
marinade, and pat dry with kitchen
paper. Melt the butter in a
flameproof casserole. Add the hare
cubes and brown on all sides. Stir in
the reserved marinade, carrots and
stock and bring to the boil. Cover
and cook in a preheated moderate
oven, 180°C (350°F), Gas Mark 4, for
2 hours.

Meanwhile, blanch the onions in
boiling water for 5 minutes, then
drain and peel, when cool enough to
handle.

Add the onions and mushrooms to
the casserole and stir well. Cook,
uncovered, for a further 30 minutes
or until the hare is tender. Discard
the bay leaf before serving.
Serves 4

Japanese Chicken Casserole

150 ml (¼ pint)
  chicken stock
6 tablespoons dry
  sherry
4 tablespoons soy
  sauce
1 teaspoon sugar
8 chicken pieces,
  skinned
25 g (1 oz) cornflour
1 teaspoon ground
  ginger
salt and pepper
4 tablespoons oil
2 canned water
  chestnuts, drained
  and sliced
4 spring onions,
  chopped

Mix together the stock, sherry, soy sauce and sugar in a shallow dish. Add the chicken pieces and turn to coat. Leave to marinate in the refrigerator overnight.

Drain the chicken pieces, reserving the marinade, and pat dry with kitchen paper. Mix the cornflour, ginger, salt and pepper together and use to coat the chicken. Heat the oil in a frying pan, add the chicken pieces and brown on all sides.

Cover the bottom of a greased flameproof casserole with the water chestnuts and spring onions. Drain the chicken pieces and place them on top. Pour over the marinade and bring to the boil. Cover and cook in a preheated moderate oven, 180°C (350°F), Gas Mark 4, for about 1 hour or until the chicken is tender.
Serves 4

Coq au Vin

125 g (4 oz) salt
  pork, diced
25 g (1 oz) butter
4 chicken quarters
250 g (8 oz) button
  onions
1 clove garlic,
  crushed
2 tablespoons plain
  flour
600 ml (1 pint) dry
  red wine
salt and pepper
250 g (8 oz) button
  mushrooms
150 ml (¼ pint)
  chicken stock
  (approximately)
1 bouquet garni
chopped parsley to
  garnish

Blanch the salt pork in boiling water
for 5 minutes, then drain well. Melt
the butter in a frying pan and fry the
pork until beginning to crisp.
Remove with a slotted spoon and
place in a casserole.

Add the chicken quarters to the
pan and brown on all sides, then
transfer to the casserole.

Add the onions and garlic to the
pan and cook gently until they are
beginning to soften and brown. Add
to the casserole.

Pour off all but about 2 tablespoons
of fat from the pan and stir in the
flour. Cook, stirring, for 2 minutes.
Gradually stir in the wine, bring to
the boil, then simmer, stirring, until
thickened. Season with salt and
pepper to taste and stir in the
mushrooms.

Pour the sauce over the chicken in
the casserole, adding enough stock to
cover the chicken. Add the bouquet
garni, cover and cook in a preheated
moderately hot oven, 190°C (375°F),
Gas Mark 5, for about 1 hour or
until the chicken is tender. Remove
the bouquet garni and serve
sprinkled with chopped parsley.
Serves 4

Arroz con Pollo

50 g (2 oz) butter
3 tablespoons olive
 oil
1 clove garlic,
 crushed
8 chicken pieces
400 g (14 oz)
 long-grain rice
1.5 litres (2½ pints)
 chicken stock
1 teaspoon turmeric
salt and pepper
50 g (2 oz) chorizo
 or garlic sausage,
 chopped
1 red pepper, cored,
 seeded and diced
parsley sprigs to
 garnish

Melt the butter with the oil in a flameproof casserole. Add the garlic and chicken pieces and brown on all sides. Remove the chicken pieces.

Add the rice to the casserole and stir well to mix with the fat. Fry until golden, stirring, then stir in the stock, turmeric and salt and pepper to taste. Bring to the boil.

Add the chorizo or garlic sausage and red pepper and mix well. Return the chicken pieces to the casserole and bury in the rice mixture. Cover and cook in a preheated moderate oven, 180°C (350°F), Gas Mark 4, for about 1 hour or until the chicken is tender and the rice has absorbed the liquid. Serve garnished with parsley.
Serves 4

Curried Chicken Casserole

50 g (2 oz) butter
2 large onions, finely
 chopped
1 clove garlic,
 crushed
1 green chilli, seeded
 and finely chopped
2.5 cm (1 inch) piece
 fresh root ginger,
 peeled and finely
 chopped
1 teaspoon turmeric
½ teaspoon ground
 cardamom
1 teaspoon ground
 coriander
1 teaspoon ground
 cumin
1 teaspoon salt
450 ml (¾ pint)
 plain yogurt
4 chicken quarters,
 skinned

Melt the butter in a flameproof casserole, add the onions and fry until softened. Stir in the garlic, chilli, ginger, turmeric, cardamom, coriander, cumin and salt and cook, stirring, for 5 minutes. Stir in the yogurt, then add the chicken pieces to the casserole and spoon the spice mixture over them. Cover and cook in a preheated moderate oven, 160°C (325°F), Gas Mark 3, for 1½ hours or until the chicken is tender.
Serves 4

Spring Chicken Casserole

3 tablespoons plain
  flour
1/4 teaspoon paprika
salt and pepper
8 chicken pieces
50 g (2 oz) butter
8 small new carrots,
  scraped
12 button onions
1 celery stick, cut
  into 5 cm (2 inch)
  strips
450 ml (3/4 pint)
  boiling chicken
  stock
1 bouquet garni
3 tablespoons double
  cream

Mix the flour with the paprika and a little salt and pepper, then use to coat the chicken pieces. Melt the butter in a frying pan and brown the chicken pieces on all sides, then transfer to a casserole.

Add the carrots, onions and celery to the fat in the pan and fry until just golden. Add to the chicken. Pour over the stock and add the bouquet garni. Cover and cook in a preheated moderate oven, 180°C (350°F), Gas Mark 4, for about 1 1/4 hours or until the chicken and vegetables are tender. Discard the bouquet garni. Stir in the cream just before serving.
Serves 4

Welsh Chicken Casserole

500 g (1 lb) leeks
500 g (1 lb) cooked
    chicken meat, cut
    into strips
65 g (2½ oz) butter
50 g (2 oz) plain
    flour
300 ml (½ pint)
    chicken stock
300 ml (½ pint)
    milk
¼ teaspoon dry
    mustard
salt and pepper
75 g (3 oz)
    Caerphilly or
    Cheddar cheese,
    grated
25 g (1 oz) dry
    breadcrumbs

Halve the leeks crossways, then cut into quarters lengthways. Place in a greased casserole and arrange the chicken on top.

Melt 50 g (2 oz) of the butter in a saucepan. Add the flour and cook, stirring, for 2 minutes. Gradually stir in the stock and milk. Bring to the boil, then simmer, stirring, until thickened. Add the mustard, salt and pepper to taste and the cheese and stir until melted. Pour this sauce over the chicken and leeks.

Melt the remaining butter and mix with the breadcrumbs. Scatter over the top of the casserole. Cook in a preheated moderate oven, 180°C (350°F), Gas Mark 4, for 30 minutes.
Serves 4

Illustrated above:
Welsh chicken casserole;
Grapefruit chicken
(page 64).

Grapefruit Chicken

8 chicken breasts,
  skinned
salt and pepper
25 g (1 oz) butter
1 tablespoon oil
1 large onion, sliced
1 teaspoon grated
  grapefruit rind
175 ml (6 fl oz)
  fresh grapefruit
  juice
3 tablespoons honey
grapefruit segments
  to garnish

Rub the chicken breasts with salt and pepper. Melt the butter with the oil in a frying pan and fry the chicken pieces until browned on all sides. Transfer to a casserole.

Add the onion to the fat remaining in the pan and fry until softened. Arrange the onion over the chicken.

Mix together the grapefruit rind and juice, honey and salt and pepper to taste, then pour over the chicken pieces. Cover and cook in a preheated moderate oven, 180°C (350°F), Gas Mark 4, for 1¼ to 1½ hours or until the chicken is cooked through. Serve garnished with grapefruit segments.

Serves 4

Illustrated on page 63.

Smothered Chicken

50 g (2 oz) plain
  flour
salt and pepper
8 chicken pieces
50 g (2 oz) butter
1 onion, finely
  chopped
1 small carrot, diced
1 small celery stick,
  finely chopped
450 ml (¾ pint)
  chicken stock
6 tablespoons double
  cream

Season half the flour and use to coat the chicken pieces. Melt the butter in a frying pan and add the chicken pieces. Brown on all sides, then transfer to a casserole.

Add the onion, carrot and celery to the fat remaining in the pan and fry until the onion is softened. Sprinkle over the remaining flour and cook, stirring, for 3 minutes. Gradually stir in the stock and bring to the boil. Simmer, stirring, until thickened, then pour over the chicken.

Cover and cook in a preheated moderate oven, 180°C (350°F), Gas Mark 4, for about 1 hour or until the chicken is tender.

Transfer the chicken pieces to a warmed serving dish and keep hot. Stir the cream into the sauce in the casserole and adjust the seasoning. Pour over the chicken.

Serves 4

Citrus Chicken

4 chicken quarters,
  skinned
salt and pepper
ground cinnamon
2 large lemons or
  limes
2 large oranges
25 g (1 oz) butter
parsley sprigs to
  garnish

Rub the chicken quarters with salt and pepper and a little cinnamon. Place in a greased casserole.

Squeeze the juice from one of the lemons or limes and pour over the chicken. Grate the rind from one of the oranges. Peel the remaining lemon or lime and both oranges and chop the flesh. Mix the flesh with the grated orange rind and pour over the chicken. Dot with the butter.

Cover tightly and cook in a pre-heated moderately hot oven, 190°C (375°F), Gas Mark 5, for 1 hour or until tender. Garnish with parsley.
Serves 4

Chicken Pilaf

50 g (2 oz) butter
25 g (1 oz) plain
  flour
1 x 426 ml (¾ pint)
  can evaporated
  milk
300 ml (½ pint)
  chicken stock
500 g (1 lb) cooked
  chicken meat,
  diced
500 g (1 lb) cooked
  long-grain rice
125 g (4 oz)
  mushrooms, sliced
1 small green pepper,
  cored, seeded and
  diced
1 small red pepper,
  cored, seeded and
  diced
salt and pepper

Melt the butter in a saucepan. Add the flour and cook, stirring, for 2 minutes. Gradually stir in the evaporated milk and stock and bring to the boil. Simmer, stirring, until thickened.

Remove the sauce from the heat and fold in the chicken, rice, mushrooms, peppers and salt and pepper to taste. Turn into a greased casserole. Cover and cook in a preheated moderate oven, 180°C (350°F), Gas Mark 4, for 45 minutes.
Serves 6 to 8

Crispy Chicken

500 g (1 lb) cooked
  chicken meat,
  chopped
4 celery sticks,
  chopped
150 ml (¼ pint)
  mayonnaise
2 tablespoons lemon
  juice
4 spring onions,
  finely chopped
25 g (1 oz) slivered
  almonds, toasted
50 g (2 oz) mature
  Cheddar cheese,
  grated
salt and pepper
50 g (2 oz) crisps,
  crushed

Mix together the chicken, celery, mayonnaise, lemon juice, spring onions, almonds, cheese and salt and pepper to taste. Turn into a casserole. Sprinkle the crisps over the top and cook in a preheated moderately hot oven, 200°C (400°F), Gas Mark 6, for 25 to 30 minutes or until piping hot.
Serves 4

Chicken with Sour Cream and Mushrooms

50 g (2 oz) butter
125 g (4 oz)
  mushrooms, sliced
25 g (1 oz) plain
  flour
150 ml (¼ pint) dry
  white wine
300 ml (½ pint)
  milk (or mixed
  milk and single
  cream)
150 ml (¼ pint)
  fresh sour cream
grated nutmeg
salt and pepper
8 chicken breasts,
  skinned
chopped parsley to
  garnish

Melt the butter in a saucepan, add the mushrooms and sauté until just tender. Remove from the pan with a slotted spoon and set aside.

Add the flour to the fat remaining in the pan and cook, stirring, for 1 minute. Gradually stir in the wine and milk (or milk and cream) and bring to the boil. Simmer, stirring, until thickened. Add half the mushrooms to the sauce, with the sour cream, and season to taste with nutmeg, salt and pepper.

Arrange the chicken breasts in a casserole. Pour over the sauce. Cover and cook in a preheated moderate oven, 180°C (350°F), Gas Mark 4, for 1¼ to 1½ hours or until the chicken is tender. Serve garnished with the remaining mushrooms and parsley.
Serves 4

Spicy Chicken with Fruit

3 tablespoons plain
  flour
salt and pepper
4 chicken quarters
50 g (2 oz) butter
1 onion, thinly sliced
1 tablespoon chilli
  seasoning (or more
  to taste)
1 x 227 g (8 oz) can
  tomatoes
150 ml (¼ pint)
  chicken stock
2 fresh peaches,
  peeled, stoned and
  sliced (or use
  canned peach
  slices)
3 bananas, thinly
  sliced

Season the flour and use to coat the chicken quarters. Melt the butter in a frying pan and brown the chicken quarters on all sides, then transfer to a casserole.

Add the onion to the pan and fry until softened. Stir in the chilli seasoning, tomatoes with their juice, and stock. Bring to the boil. Season with salt and pepper to taste and stir in the peaches and bananas. Pour this mixture over the chicken quarters.

Cover and cook in a preheated moderate oven, 180°C (350°F), Gas Mark 4, for 1¼ to 1½ hours or until the chicken is tender.
Serves 4

VEGETABLES

Tomatoes with Parmesan and Cream

8 large tomatoes,
  skinned and sliced
3 tablespoons
  medium sherry
½ teaspoon sugar
salt and pepper
25 g (1 oz)
  Parmesan cheese,
  grated
150 ml (¼ pint)
  double cream
parsley sprigs to
  garnish

Arrange the tomato slices in a greased small casserole. Sprinkle with the sherry, sugar and salt and pepper to taste, then the Parmesan. Pour the cream over the top.

Cook in a preheated moderately hot oven, 200°C (400°F), Gas Mark 6, for about 20 minutes. Serve garnished with parsley sprigs.
Serves 4

Aubergine and bacon casserole; Tomatoes with Parmesan and cream; Broccoli lorraine (page 72).

Aubergine and Bacon Casserole

750 g (1½ lb)
  aubergines, cut
  into 1 cm
  (½ inch) slices
salt and pepper
5 tablespoons oil
  (approximately)
250 g (8 oz) streaky
  bacon rashers,
  derinded and diced
1 large onion,
  chopped
1 clove garlic, crushed
1 medium green
  pepper, cored,
  seeded and diced
250 g (8 oz)
  mushrooms, sliced
1 x 397 g (14 oz)
  can tomatoes
½ teaspoon dried
  thyme
1 teaspoon sugar
125 g (4 oz)
  Mozzarella or
  Gruyère cheese,
  shredded

Sprinkle the aubergine slices with salt and leave to drain for 30 minutes. Rinse and pat dry.

Brush a baking sheet with a little of the oil and arrange the aubergine slices on top in a single layer. Brush with the remaining oil. Cook in a preheated hot oven, 230°C (450°F), Gas Mark 8, for 35 minutes.

Meanwhile, fry the bacon in a frying pan until crisp, then remove.

Add the onion, garlic and green pepper to the pan and fry until the onion is softened. Stir in the mushrooms, tomatoes, with their juice, thyme, salt and pepper to taste and the sugar. Simmer until quite thick, stirring occasionally.

Layer the aubergine slices, bacon and tomato sauce in a shallow casserole. Top with the cheese.

Reduce the oven temperature to moderate, 180°C (350°F), Gas Mark 4, and cook for 20 minutes or until beginning to brown.

Serves 4 to 6

Broccoli Lorraine

750 g (1 ½ lb)
  broccoli, cut into
  5 cm (2 inch)
  pieces
15 g (½ oz) butter
4 back bacon rashers,
  derinded and diced
1 onion, thinly sliced
300 ml (½ pint)
  milk
150 ml (¼ pint)
  single cream
4 eggs, beaten
25 g (1 oz) Gruyère
  cheese, grated
salt and pepper

Arrange the broccoli in a greased casserole. Melt the butter in a frying pan, add the bacon and fry until crisp. Remove the bacon with a slotted spoon and sprinkle on top of the broccoli.

Fry the onion in the fat remaining in the pan until golden, then remove with a slotted spoon and scatter over the broccoli.

Mix together the milk, cream, eggs, cheese and salt and pepper to taste, then pour into the casserole.

Place the casserole in a roasting pan, containing about 2.5 cm (1 inch) of boiling water. Cook in a preheated moderate oven, 180°C (350°F), Gas Mark 4, for 30 minutes or until just set.

Serves 4 to 6

Illustrated on page 71.

Swede and Apple Casserole

750 g (1 ½ lb)
  swede, cubed
salt and pepper
1 large cooking
  apple, peeled,
  cored and sliced
50 g (2 oz) brown
  sugar
25 g (1 oz) butter
3 to 4 tablespoons
  medium sherry
  (optional)

Cook the swede in boiling salted water for 20 to 30 minutes or until just tender. Drain well.

Put half the swede in a greased casserole and cover with half the apple slices. Sprinkle over half the brown sugar and salt and pepper to taste. Dot with half the butter. Repeat the layers. Sprinkle over the sherry, if using.

Cover and cook in a preheated moderate oven, 180°C (350°F), Gas Mark 4, for 30 minutes.

Serves 4

Pineapple Parsnips

1 kg (1 lb) parsnips,
  quartered
  lengthways
150 ml (¼ pint)
  unsweetened
  pineapple juice
1 teaspoon sugar
salt and pepper
40 g (1½ oz) butter

Cut the cores from the parsnips, then place in a greased baking dish. Mix together the pineapple juice, sugar and salt and pepper to taste and pour over the parsnips. Dot with the butter. Cover and cook in a preheated moderate oven, 180°C (350°F), Gas Mark 4, for 1 hour or until the parsnips are tender.

Serves 4

Green Peppers and Beans

500 g (1 lb) runner
    beans (stringed if
    necessary)
2 green peppers,
    cored, seeded and
    chopped
2 onions, finely
    chopped
salt and pepper
dried thyme
40 g (1½ oz) butter

If the beans are large, cut in half.
Make alternate layers of the
vegetables in a greased casserole,
beginning and ending with beans.
Sprinkle each layer with salt and
pepper and a little thyme and dot
with butter.

Cover tightly and cook in a
preheated moderate oven, 180°C
(350°F), Gas Mark 4, for 1 hour or
until the vegetables are very tender.
Serves 4

74

Red Cabbage with Apple

1 kg (2 lb) red cabbage, cored and shredded
40 g (1½ oz) butter
1 onion, sliced
2 medium cooking apples, peeled, cored and sliced
3 tablespoons water
3 tablespoons wine vinegar
4 teaspoons sugar
salt and pepper
15 g (½ oz) plain flour
chopped parsley to garnish

Blanch the cabbage in boiling water for 1 minute, then drain well. Melt 25 g (1 oz) of the butter in a flameproof casserole. Add the onion and fry until softened. Add the apples and fry for a further 5 minutes. Remove from the casserole with a slotted spoon.

Make alternate layers of the cabbage and apple mixture in the casserole, beginning and ending with cabbage. Sprinkle each layer with water, vinegar, sugar, salt and pepper. Cover tightly and cook in a preheated moderate oven, 160°C (325°F), Gas Mark 3, for 2 hours, stirring occasionally and adding more water if necessary.

Blend the remaining butter with the flour to make a paste. Mix with a little of the liquid from the casserole, then stir this into the casserole. Cook gently on top of the stove until thickened. Garnish with parsley.
Serves 4

Broad Beans with Walnuts

1 kg (2 lb) fresh broad beans, shelled
salt and pepper
25 g (1 oz) butter
1 small onion, finely chopped
150 ml (¼ pint) chicken stock
250 g (8 oz) Cheddar cheese, grated
1½ teaspoons French mustard
1 teaspoon Worcestershire sauce
125 g (4 oz) walnuts, chopped

Cook the beans in boiling salted water for 5 minutes. Drain well.

Melt the butter in a clean saucepan. Add the onion and fry until softened. Stir in the stock and bring to the boil. Add the cheese, stir until melted, then mix in the mustard, Worcestershire sauce and salt and pepper to taste. Fold in the walnuts and beans.

Turn into a greased casserole. Cook in a preheated moderate oven, 180°C (350°F), Gas Mark 4, for 30 minutes.
Serves 4

Stuffed Cabbage

1 medium cabbage
2 tablespoons olive
    oil
4 back bacon rashers,
    derinded and
    chopped
1 onion, chopped
1 clove garlic,
    crushed
1 egg, beaten
2 tablespoons grated
    Parmesan cheese
3 tablespoons
    chopped parsley
salt and pepper
250 ml (8 fl oz)
    chicken stock

Cook the whole cabbage in boiling water for 15 minutes. Drain and cool under cold running water. Cut out the core, then remove the inner cabbage leaves, leaving the outside leaves intact. Chop the inner leaves.

Heat the oil in a frying pan, add the chopped cabbage leaves, bacon, onion and garlic and fry until the onion is softened. Remove from the heat. Mix together the egg, cheese, parsley and salt and pepper to taste and stir into the cabbage mixture.

Place the cabbage 'shell' of large outside leaves in a casserole lined with foil and fill the shell with the fried mixture. Pour over the stock. Cover and cook in a preheated moderately hot oven, 190°C (375°F), Gas Mark 5, for 1 hour. Uncover the casserole and cook for a further 30 minutes. To serve, lift the cabbage out, then remove the foil.

Serves 6 to 8

Scalloped Potatoes

8 medium potatoes,
  thinly sliced
1 medium onion,
  thinly sliced
6 tablespoons plain
  flour
salt and pepper
600 ml (1 pint) milk
4 tablespoons dry
  breadcrumbs
15 g (½ oz) butter,
  melted

Make a layer of about one third of the potato slices in a greased casserole. Sprinkle with one third of the onion and flour and season with salt and pepper to taste. Repeat these layers twice, then pour over the milk.

Mix the breadcrumbs with the butter and sprinkle over the top. Cover and cook in a preheated moderate oven, 180°C (350°F), Gas Mark 4, for 1¼ hours.

Remove the lid and continue cooking for 15 minutes or until the top is crisp and golden brown.
Serves 6

Courgette Casserole

1 kg (2 lb) courgettes
salt and pepper
1 teaspoon dried
  oregano
125 g (4 oz) mature
  Double Gloucester
  cheese, grated
50 g (2 oz) blanched
  almonds, chopped
25 g (1 oz) butter,
  melted

Steam the courgettes until just tender. Cut into 1 cm (½ inch) slices and layer a quarter of these in a greased casserole. Sprinkle with salt and pepper and a quarter of the oregano. Cover with a quarter of the cheese. Continue making layers in this way, ending with cheese.

Mix together the nuts and butter and scatter over the top. Cook in a preheated moderate oven, 180°C (350°F), Gas Mark 4, for 20 minutes.
Serves 4 to 6

Sweetcorn Pudding

350 g (12 oz) frozen
  or canned sweetcorn
450 ml (¾ pint) milk
3 eggs, beaten
1 small onion, grated
1 teaspoon sugar
15 g (½ oz) butter,
  melted
salt and pepper
parsley sprigs to
  garnish

If using frozen sweetcorn, allow it to thaw; drain canned sweetcorn. Mix together all the ingredients with salt and pepper to taste. Turn into a greased casserole. Place in a baking tin containing 2.5 cm (1 inch) water.

Cook in a preheated moderate oven, 180°C (350°F), Gas Mark 4, for about 45 minutes or until a knife inserted into the centre comes out clean. Garnish with parsley.
Serves 4 to 6

Spinach and Bacon Bake

750 g (1½ lb)
  spinach
4 unsmoked streaky
  bacon rashers,
  derinded and diced
125 g (4 oz)
  mushrooms, sliced
salt and pepper
½ teaspoon dried
  thyme
300 ml (½) pint
  fresh sour cream
25 g (1 oz) mature
  Cheddar cheese,
  grated
25 g (1 oz)
  Parmesan cheese,
  grated

Cook the spinach, with just the water clinging to the leaves after washing, until tender. Drain well, pressing out all the excess moisture, then chop. Spread the chopped spinach over the bottom of a greased casserole.

Fry the bacon in a dry frying pan until crisp. Drain on kitchen paper and sprinkle over the spinach. Cover with the mushrooms, then season with salt and pepper to taste and sprinkle with the thyme. Cook in a preheated moderate oven, 160°C (325°F), Gas Mark 3, for 15 minutes.

Pour over the cream. Mix together the Parmesan and Cheddar cheese and scatter over the top. Return to the oven and cook for a further 10 minutes or until the cheese is melted.
Serves 4 to 6

Fettucine Casserole

250 g (8 oz) green
noodles (fettucine
verde)
salt and pepper
2 tablespoons olive oil
1 onion, chopped
1 clove garlic,
crushed (optional)
125 g (4 oz)
mushrooms, sliced
250 g (8 oz) Italian
garlic sausage,
finely chopped
250 g (8 oz) Ricotta
or curd cheese
1 egg
125 g (4 oz)
Mozzarella or
Gruyère cheese,
shredded

Cook the noodles in boiling salted water until just tender.

Meanwhile, heat the oil in a frying pan, add the onion and garlic (if using) and fry until softened. Add the mushrooms and fry for a further 3 minutes, then stir in the sausage. Remove from the heat.

Drain the noodles and fold into the sausage mixture. Beat the Ricotta cheese and egg together and stir into the sausage mixture with salt and pepper to taste. Turn into a casserole and top with the Mozzarella cheese. Bake in a preheated moderate oven, 160°C (325°F), Gas Mark 3, for 35 minutes.
Serves 4

Macaroni cheese with sour cream; Fettucine casserole; Lasagne (page 82).

Macaroni Cheese with Sour Cream

250 g (8 oz)
  macaroni
salt and pepper
25 g (1 oz) butter,
  melted
125 g (4 oz) mature
  Cheddar cheese,
  grated
150 ml (¼ pint)
  fresh sour cream
4 tablespoons milk
1 egg, beaten
pinch of paprika

Cook the macaroni in boiling salted water until tender. Drain well, then mix with the butter and salt and pepper to taste. Make alternate layers of macaroni and cheese in a casserole, reserving about 2 tablespoons of the cheese for the topping.

Mix together the sour cream, milk, egg, paprika and salt and pepper to taste. Pour over the macaroni and scatter the remaining cheese on top. Cook in a preheated moderately hot oven, 200°C (400°F), Gas Mark 6, for about 20 minutes or until the top is golden brown.

Serves 4

Lasagne

2 tablespoons olive oil
2 onions, chopped
1 clove garlic, crushed
750 g (1 ½ lb)
    minced beef
2 x 397 g (14 oz)
    cans tomatoes
4 tablespoons tomato
    purée
150 ml (¼ pint) water
1 ½ teaspoons sugar
2 teaspoons dried
    mixed herbs
1 bay leaf
salt and pepper
250 g (8 oz)
    mushrooms, sliced
500 g (1 lb) lasagne
500 g (1 lb) Ricotta
    or curd cheese
500 g (1 lb) Mozza-
    rella or Gruyère
    cheese, sliced
250 g (8 oz)
    Parmesan cheese,
    grated

Heat the oil in a frying pan, add the onions and garlic and fry until softened. Add the beef and fry until well browned, then stir in the tomatoes with their juice, tomato purée, water, sugar, herbs and salt and pepper to taste. Bring to the boil and simmer gently for 1 ¼ hours. Stir in the mushrooms and simmer for 20 minutes. Discard the bay leaf.

Just before the sauce is ready, cook the lasagne, in batches, in boiling salted water. (A little oil added to the water will prevent the sheets of pasta sticking together.) Drain well.

Spoon a little of the sauce over the bottom of a shallow baking dish. Cover with a layer of lasagne, then a layer each of the Ricotta, Mozzarella and Parmesan cheeses. Continue making layers in this way, ending with lasagne sprinkled with Parmesan. Cook in a preheated moderate oven, 180°C (350°F), Gas Mark 4, for 1 hour.
Serves 8 to 10

Illustrated on page 81.

Noodles Paprika

175 g (6 oz) noodles
salt and pepper
15 g (½ oz) butter
1 medium onion,
    finely chopped
1 clove garlic,
    crushed
2 teaspoons paprika
250 g (8 oz) cottage
    cheese
300 ml (½ pint)
    fresh sour cream
few drops of Tabasco
    sauce
1 teaspoon caraway
    seeds (optional)
paprika to garnish

Cook the noodles in boiling salted water until just tender. Drain well. Melt the butter in a frying pan, add the onion and garlic and fry until softened. Stir in the paprika. Cook, stirring, for 1 minute.

Remove from the heat and stir in the cottage cheese, sour cream, Tabasco and salt and pepper to taste. Add the caraway seeds (if using). Fold in the noodles.

Turn into a greased casserole and cook in a preheated moderate oven, 180°C (350°F), Gas Mark 4, for 30 minutes. Sprinkle with paprika to garnish.
Serves 4 to 6

Cheese Charlotte

75 g (3 oz) butter
12 x 1 cm (½ inch)
  thick slices white
  bread, crusts
  removed
125 g (4 oz) mature
  Cheddar cheese,
  grated
350 ml (12 fl oz)
  milk
2 eggs, beaten
salt and pepper
pinch of dry mustard
2 tablespoons
  chopped fresh
  chives

Butter all the bread slices. Cut 4 or 5 slices into 2.5 cm (1 inch) wide fingers and use to line a deep, straight-sided casserole, buttered side against the casserole. Cut the remaining slices into cubes.

Make alternate layers of bread cubes and grated cheese in the casserole. Mix together the milk, eggs, salt and pepper to taste, mustard and chives and pour into the casserole.

Cook in a preheated moderate oven, 180°C (350°F), Gas Mark 4, for 30 minutes.

Serves 4

Italian Baked Beans

500 g (1 lb) dried
  white haricot
  beans, soaked
  overnight
125 g (4 oz) Italian
  garlic sausage,
  chopped
2 cloves garlic,
  crushed
2 teaspoons dried
  oregano
salt and pepper
4 tablespoons tomato
  purée
600 ml (1 pint)
  water
  (approximately)

Drain the beans and mix with the
sausage, garlic, oregano and salt and
pepper to taste. Mix the tomato
purée with the water.

Put the bean mixture in a casserole
and stir in enough water to just
cover the beans.

Cover and cook in a preheated
cool oven, 140°C (275°F), Gas Mark
1, for 3 to 3½ hours or until the
beans are tender. If necessary, add a
little more water to the casserole
during cooking.

Serves 6

Boston Baked Beans

500 g (1 lb) dried
  haricot beans,
  soaked overnight
2 litres (3½ pints)
  water
salt and pepper
75 g (3 oz) dark
  brown sugar
1 teaspoon dry
  mustard
6 tablespoons dark
  treacle
125 g (4 oz) salt
  pork, chopped
1 medium onion,
  chopped

Drain the beans and put in a
saucepan with the water and
½ teaspoon salt. Bring to the boil,
then cover and simmer for about
1 hour or until the beans are tender.
Drain, reserving the liquid.

Mix together the sugar, mustard,
treacle, 600 ml (1 pint) of the
reserved cooking liquid and salt and
pepper to taste. Put the beans, salt
pork and onion in a casserole and stir
in the treacle mixture.

Cover and cook in a preheated
cool oven, 150°C (300°F), Gas Mark
2, for 4 hours, stirring occasionally
and adding more of the reserved
cooking liquid if necessary, during
cooking.

Serves 6 to 8

Curried Rice

250 g (8 oz)
   long-grain rice
1 litre (1 ³⁄4 pints)
   water
1 onion, finely
   chopped
2 celery sticks,
   coarsely chopped
250 g (8 oz)
   tomatoes, skinned
   and chopped
1 ½ teaspoons salt
1 ½ teaspoons mild
   curry powder (or
   more to taste)
50 g (2 oz) butter,
   melted

Put the rice in a casserole and pour over the water. Leave to soak for 45 minutes.

Stir the remaining ingredients into the rice. Cook in a preheated moderate oven, 180°C (350°F), Gas Mark 4, for 1½ hours or until the rice is tender and all the liquid has been absorbed.

Serves 6

Layered Lentil Casserole

500 g (1 lb) lentils,
  soaked overnight
1 bay leaf
6 slices cooked ham
  or gammon, cut
  into strips
1 teaspoon dried
  thyme
salt and pepper
350 g (12 oz) cooked
  chicken meat, cut
  into strips
300 ml (½ pint)
  chicken stock
  (approximately)
25 g (1 oz)
  Parmesan cheese,
  grated
25 g (1 oz) dry
  breadcrumbs

Drain the lentils and put into a saucepan with the bay leaf. Add fresh water to cover and bring to the boil. Simmer gently for about 1 hour or until tender. Drain the lentils, discarding the bay leaf.

Put about one third of the lentils in a greased casserole. Cover with the ham and sprinkle with half the thyme and salt and pepper to taste. Cover with another third of the lentils, then add the chicken. Sprinkle with the rest of the thyme and salt and pepper to taste.

Top with the remaining lentils and pour in the stock. Cover and cook in a preheated moderate oven, 180°C (350°F), Gas Mark 4, for 30 minutes.

Mix together the cheese and breadcrumbs and sprinkle over the top. Cook, uncovered, for 15 minutes or until the topping is golden brown.
Serves 4 to 6

Haricot Bean and Sweetcorn Casserole

250 g (8 oz) dried
  haricot beans,
  soaked overnight
1 x 326 g (11½ oz)
  can sweetcorn,
  drained
1 x 397 g (14 oz)
  can tomatoes,
  drained
salt and pepper
1 tablespoon brown
  sugar
1 tablespoon grated
  onion
50 g (2 oz) browned
  breadcrumbs

Drain the beans and place in a saucepan. Cover with fresh water, bring to the boil and simmer for 45 minutes or until tender.

Drain the beans and mix with the sweetcorn, tomatoes, salt and pepper to taste, sugar and onion. Turn into a greased casserole and sprinkle the breadcrumbs over the top. Cook in a preheated moderate oven, 180°C (350°F), Gas Mark 4, for 45 minutes.
Serves 4

Fruit and Nut Pilaf

75 g (3 oz) sultanas
175 g (6 oz) dried
  fruit (apricots,
  apples, pears, etc.)
1 tablespoon sweet
  sherry
75 g (3 oz) butter
1 onion, finely
  chopped
250 g (8 oz)
  long-grain rice,
  cooked
½ teaspoon ground
  allspice
salt and pepper
50 g (2 oz) flaked
  almonds

Put the sultanas and dried fruit in a bowl, sprinkle with the sherry and cover with water. Leave to soak for 4 hours. Drain and chop the apricots, apples or pears.

Melt the butter in a frying pan, add the onion and fry until softened. Stir in the rice and allspice, then add salt and pepper to taste and mix well.

Fold in the fruit and almonds, then turn the mixture into a greased casserole. Bake in a preheated moderately hot oven, 190°C (375°F), Gas Mark 5, for 30 minutes.
Serves 6

Rice with Parsley and Cheese

350 g (12 oz) cooked
long-grain rice
6 spring onions,
finely chopped
40 g (1 ½ oz)
chopped parsley
3 eggs, beaten
4 tablespoons milk
125 g (4 oz)
Cheddar cheese,
grated
salt and pepper

Mix together the rice, spring onions and parsley. Combine the remaining ingredients with salt and pepper to taste and add to the rice mixture. Blend well, then turn into a greased casserole. Cook in a preheated moderate oven, 180°C (350°F), Gas Mark 4, for 30 minutes or until just set.
Serves 4

Pearl Barley Casserole

50 g (2 oz) butter
2 medium leeks,
thinly sliced
1 green pepper,
cored, seeded and
chopped
225 g (7 oz) pearl
barley, soaked
overnight
50 g (2 oz) cooked
ham, diced
(optional)
1 x 326 g (11½ oz)
can sweetcorn,
drained
300 ml (½ pint)
chicken stock
salt and pepper

Melt the butter in a flameproof casserole. Add the leeks and green pepper and fry until softened. Drain the pearl barley and add to the casserole. Stir in the remaining ingredients with salt and pepper to taste.

Cover and cook in a preheated moderate oven, 160°C (325°F), Gas Mark 3, for 40 minutes or until the barley is tender and all the liquid absorbed.
Serves 4

Spanish Rice Casserole

5 tablespoons olive
   oil
1 onion, finely
   chopped
1 clove garlic,
   crushed
250 g (8 oz)
   long-grain rice
1 tablespoon chilli
   powder (or to
   taste)
salt and pepper
125 g (4 oz) chorizo
   or garlic sausage,
   diced
125 g (4 oz) small
   button mushrooms
450 ml (¾ pint)
   boiling stock
   (approximately)

Heat the oil in a flameproof
casserole, add the onion and garlic
and fry until softened. Stir in the
rice, chilli powder and salt and
pepper to taste. Cook, stirring, until
the rice is golden. Add the chorizo or
garlic sausage and mushrooms and
mix well. Add enough stock to come
about 2.5 cm (1 inch) above the level
of the rice; stir thoroughly.

Cover tightly and cook in a
preheated moderate oven, 180°C
(350°F), Gas Mark 4, for 30 minutes
or until the rice is tender and the
liquid absorbed.

Serves 4

INDEX